It's another winner from the CGP lab...

There are only three ways to make sure you're fully prepared for the Grade 9-1 GCSE Combined Science exams — practice, practice and practice.

That's why we've packed this brilliant CGP book with realistic exam-style questions for every topic, and we've got all the practicals covered too.

And since you'll be tested on a wide range of topics in the real exams, we've also included sections of mixed questions for Biology, Chemistry and Physics!

CGP — still the best! ☺

Our sole aim here at CGP is to produce the highest quality books — carefully written, immaculately presented and dangerously close to being funny.

Then we work our socks off to get them out to you — at the cheapest possible prices.

Contents

Use the tick boxes to check off the topics you've completed.

Section 11 — States of Matter and Mixtures

Section 12 — Chemical Changes

Section 13 — Extracting Metals and Equilibria

Section 14 — Groups in the Periodic Table

Section 15 — Rates of Reaction and Energy Changes

Section 16 — Fuels and Earth Science

Section 17 — Motion, Forces and Conservation of Energy

Section 18 — Waves and the Electromagnetic Spectrum

Published by CGP

Editors: Alex Billings, Katie Braid, Katherine Faudemer, Robin Flello, Emily Forsberg, Emily Garrett, Emily Howe, Rachel Kordan, Duncan Lindsay, Ciara McGlade, Frances Rooney, Hayley Thompson, Sarah Williams

Contributors: Mark Edwards, Alison Popperwell

With thanks to Susan Alexander, Sharon Keeley-Holden, Sarah Pattison, Peter Rich, Rachael Rogers and Jamie Sinclair for the proofreading. With thanks to Jan Greenway for the copyright research.

ISBN: 978 1 78294 499 7

Percentile Growth Chart on page 12 copyright © 2009 Royal College of Paediatrics and Child Health.

Definition of health in answers: Preamble to the Constitution of the World Health Organization as adopted by the International Health Conference, New York, 19 June - 22 July 1946; signed on 22 July 1946 by the representatives of 61 States (Official Records of the World Health Organization, no. 2, p. 100) and entered into force on 7 April 1948.

Page 63 contains public sector information published by the Health and Safety Executive and licensed under the Open Government Licence. http://www.nationalarchives.gov.uk/doc/open-government-licence/version/3/

Data provided to construct the graph on page 126 provided by The European Environment Agency.

Printed by Elanders Ltd, Newcastle upon Tyne
Clipart from Corel®
Illustrations by: Sandy Gardner Artist, email sandy@sandygardner.co.uk
Based on the classic CGP style created by Richard Parsons.

How to Use This Book

- Hold the book <u>upright</u>, approximately <u>50 cm</u> from your face, ensuring that the text looks like <u>this</u>, not this.

- In case of emergency, press the two halves of the book together <u>firmly</u> in order to close.

- Before attempting to use this book, read the following <u>safety information</u>:

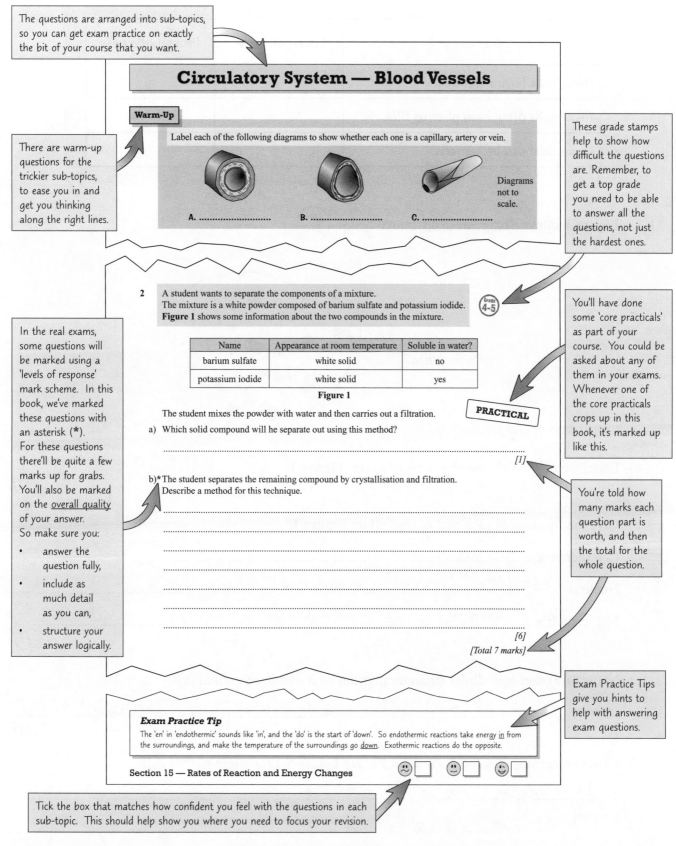

The questions are arranged into sub-topics, so you can get exam practice on exactly the bit of your course that you want.

There are warm-up questions for the trickier sub-topics, to ease you in and get you thinking along the right lines.

In the real exams, some questions will be marked using a 'levels of response' mark scheme. In this book, we've marked these questions with an asterisk (*). For these questions there'll be quite a few marks up for grabs. You'll also be marked on the <u>overall quality</u> of your answer. So make sure you:
- answer the question fully,
- include as much detail as you can,
- structure your answer logically.

These grade stamps help to show how difficult the questions are. Remember, to get a top grade you need to be able to answer all the questions, not just the hardest ones.

You'll have done some 'core practicals' as part of your course. You could be asked about any of them in your exams. Whenever one of the core practicals crops up in this book, it's marked up like this.

You're told how many marks each question part is worth, and then the total for the whole question.

Exam Practice Tips give you hints to help with answering exam questions.

Circulatory System — Blood Vessels

Warm-Up

Label each of the following diagrams to show whether each one is a capillary, artery or vein.

Diagrams not to scale.

A. ....   B. ....   C. ....

2   A student wants to separate the components of a mixture.
The mixture is a white powder composed of barium sulfate and potassium iodide.
Figure 1 shows some information about the two compounds in the mixture.

Name	Appearance at room temperature	Soluble in water?
barium sulfate	white solid	no
potassium iodide	white solid	yes

Figure 1

The student mixes the powder with water and then carries out a filtration.

a) Which solid compound will he separate out using this method?

....
[1]

b)* The student separates the remaining compound by crystallisation and filtration.
Describe a method for this technique.

....

....

....

....

....

....
[6]
[Total 7 marks]

PRACTICAL

Grade 4-5

Exam Practice Tip
The 'en' in 'endothermic' sounds like 'in', and the 'do' is the start of 'down'. So endothermic reactions take energy <u>in</u> from the surroundings, and make the temperature of the surroundings go <u>down</u>. Exothermic reactions do the opposite.

Section 15 — Rates of Reaction and Energy Changes

Tick the box that matches how confident you feel with the questions in each sub-topic. This should help show you where you need to focus your revision.

- There's also a Physics Equations List at the back of this book — you'll be given these equations in your exam. You can look up equations on this list to help you answer some of the physics questions in this book.

Cells

Warm-Up

Complete the table to show whether each statement is **true** for eukaryotic cells or prokaryotic cells. Tick **one** box in each row.

Statement	Eukaryotic cells	Prokaryotic cells
These cells have a nucleus.		
These cells often have plasmid DNA.		
These cells can be bacteria.		

1 **Figure 1** shows a diagram of an animal cell.

Figure 1

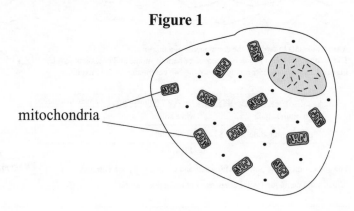

mitochondria

a) Label the cell membrane and the nucleus on **Figure 1**.

[2]

b) Give the function of each part of the cell on **Figure 1**.

Cell membrane ...Controls what goes in and out...

Nucleus ...Stores the DNA of the cell...

Mitochondria ...where respiration takes place...

[3]

c) Name **one** other subcellular structure that can be found in an animal cell.
...Another subcellular structure is cytoplasm...

[1]

d) Give **two** reasons why the diagram in **Figure 1** does not represent a plant cell.

1. It does not contain a cell wall

2. Does not contain chlorophyll

[2]

[Total 8 marks]

Specialised Cells

1 A sperm cell is specialised for its function. (Grade 3-4)

a) What is the function of a sperm cell?

...To ~~a~~ merge ~~in~~ the egg cell......................................

[1]

Figure 1 shows a sperm cell.

Figure 1

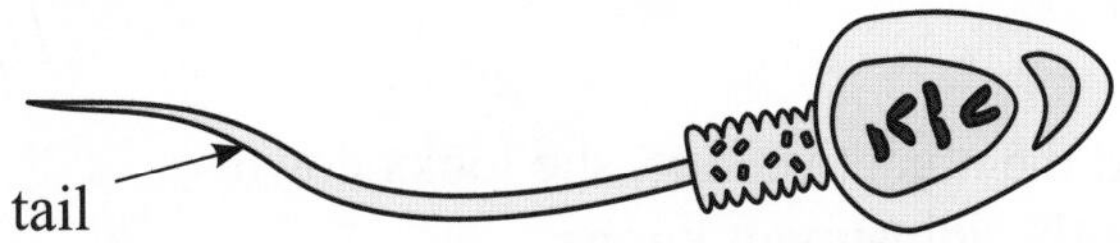

tail

b) State how the sperm cell's **tail** helps it to carry out its function.

...The tail) allows the cell to move ~~around~~....

[1]

c) State **one** other feature of a sperm cell and explain how it helps the cell to carry out its function.

...Another feature is the nucleus or

the sperm and egg cells fuse together

[2]

[Total 4 marks]

2 An egg cell is fertilised when the nucleus of an egg cell and the nucleus of a sperm cell fuse together. Both egg cells and sperm cells are haploid. (Grade 4-5)

a) Elephant body cells contain 56 chromosomes.
How many chromosomes will an elephant egg cell contain?

...Each cell will contain 28 chromosomes

[1]

b) Explain why the membrane of an egg cell changes its structure immediately after fertilisation.

...The membrane of an egg cell changes structure

as it stops more sperm getting in so only one

sperm can fertilise the egg

[2]

c) State how the cytoplasm of an egg cell is adapted to its function.

....

....

[1]

[Total 4 marks]

Microscopy

1 A student wants to use a light microscope to view a sample of onion cells. **Figure 1** shows a diagram of the light microscope that she plans to use.

Grade 4-5

a) i) The three different objective lenses are labelled in **Figure 1** with their magnification.

Which lens should the student select first when viewing her cells?

...............Light...microscopes...............
[1]

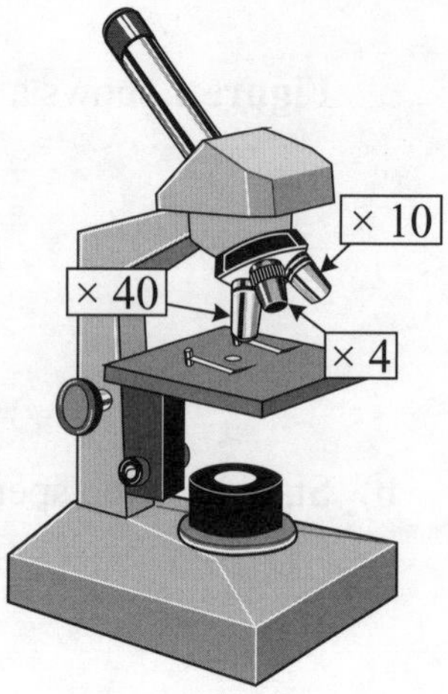

ii) After she has selected the objective lens, she looks down the eyepiece and uses the adjustment knobs.

Describe the purpose of the adjustment knobs.

.......Use...the...coarse...adjustment...knob...
...to...move...the...stage...up...to...just.......
...underneath...the...objective...lens.......
[1]

Figure 1

× 10
× 40
× 4

iii) The student wants to see the cells at a greater magnification.

Describe the steps that she should take.

.......If...the...student...wants...to...make...the...............
...image...bigger...use...an...objective...lens.......
...with...a...higher...magnification...and...refocus.......
[2]

b) After she has viewed the cells, she wants to produce a scientific drawing of them. Her teacher has told her to use smooth lines to draw the structures she can see.

Give **two** other things the student should do to produce a useful scientific drawing.

1. ....Dont...do...any...colouring...or...shading.......
2. ....Include...the...magnification...used...and...a...scale.......
[2]

c) The student compares the image that she can see with an image of onion cells viewed with an electron microscope.

Describe **one** difference that the student could expect to see between the two images.

.......Electron...microscopes...can...make...specimens.......
...look...bigger...and...show...more...detail...than...light.......
...microscopes.......
[1]

[Total 7 marks]

More Microscopy

Warm-Up

Put the measurements on the right in order, from smallest to largest.

smallest ....4.9nm....   **5 mm**

....6 μm....   **4.9 nm**

largest ....5mm....   **6 μm**

1   A sample of epithelial cells were viewed using a light microscope.

Figure 1 shows the magnification of the lenses used to view the cells.

Figure 1

Lens	Magnification
Eyepiece lens	× 10
Objective lens	× 100

a) What was the total magnification used to view the cells?

☐ **A** × 110   ☐ **B** × 90   ☐ **C** × 10 000   ☑ **D** × 1000

[1]

Figure 2 shows an image of one of the cells.
A scale is included with the image.

Figure 2

b) What is the real height of the cell?

☐ **A** 10 μm   ☑ **C** 25 μm

☐ **B** 15 μm   ☐ **D** 40 μm

[1]
[Total 2 marks]

10 μm

2   A plant cell is magnified under a light microscope.
In the image, the plant cell is 4 mm long. The real length of the plant cell is 0.01 mm.

Calculate the magnification the plant cell was viewed under.

magnification = ...
[Total 2 marks]

Enzymes

1 **Figure 1** shows an enzyme. (Grade 1-3)

Figure 1

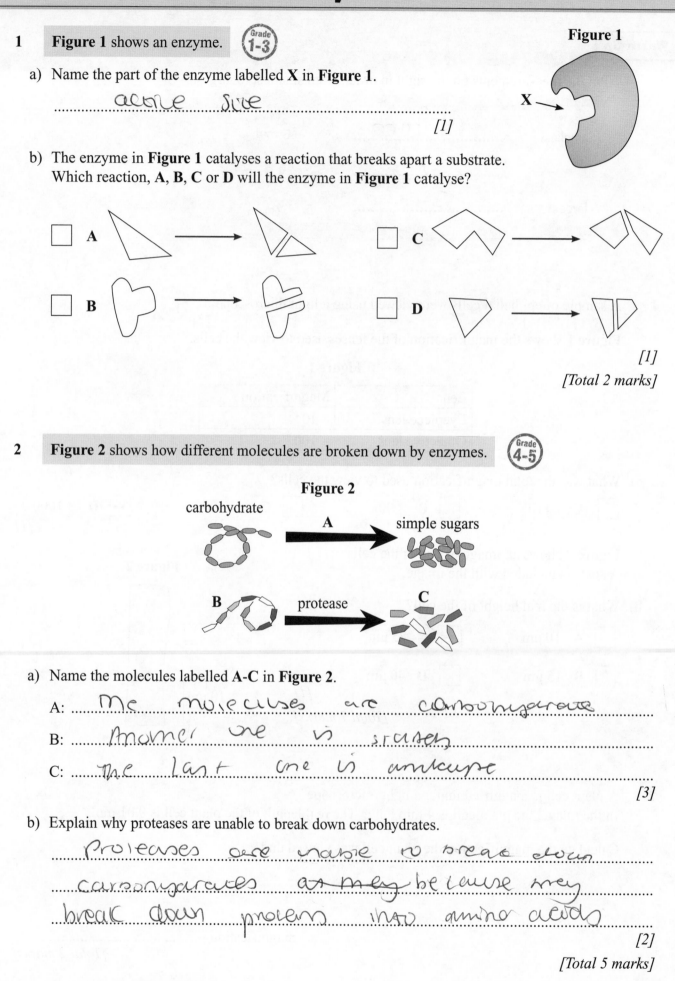

a) Name the part of the enzyme labelled **X** in **Figure 1**.

.... active site ....

[1]

b) The enzyme in **Figure 1** catalyses a reaction that breaks apart a substrate. Which reaction, **A**, **B**, **C** or **D** will the enzyme in **Figure 1** catalyse?

☐ **A**

☐ **B**

☐ **C**

☐ **D**

[1]

[Total 2 marks]

2 **Figure 2** shows how different molecules are broken down by enzymes. (Grade 4-5)

Figure 2

carbohydrate → **A** → simple sugars

B → protease → **C**

a) Name the molecules labelled **A-C** in **Figure 2**.

A: ...... The molecules are carbohydrate ......

B: ...... Another one is starch ......

C: ...... The last one is amylase ......

[3]

b) Explain why proteases are unable to break down carbohydrates.

...... Proteases are unable to break down ......
...... carbohydrates as they because they ......
...... break down protein into amino acids ......

[2]

[Total 5 marks]

Section 1 — Key Concepts in Biology

☹ ☐   😐 ☐   🙂 ☐

Factors Affecting Enzyme Activity

1 A student is investigating how the concentration of substrate molecules affects the rate of an enzyme-controlled reaction. *Grade 3-4*

Use words from the box to complete the passage below.

| decreases | increases | doesn't change | denatured | full |

At first, as substrate concentration increases, the rate of the reaction ......increases...... .

Once all the active sites are ....full......, increasing the substrate concentration
.....doesn't change..... the rate of the reaction.

[Total 3 marks]

2 A reaction is catalysed by an enzyme. **Figure 1** shows how temperature affects the rate of this reaction. *Grade 4-5*

Figure 1

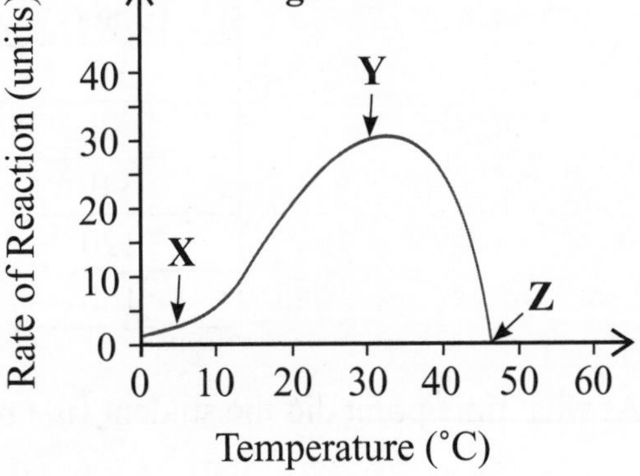

a) Look at points **X** and **Y** on **Figure 1**.

Describe the relationship between rate of reaction and temperature between points **X** and **Y**.

It it gets to hot sume or the bonds holding
the enzyme together break *[1]*

b) Using **Figure 1**, estimate the optimum temperature for this reaction.

The optimum pressure is 36 *[1]*

c) Explain why the reaction has stopped at point **Z**.

The reaction had stopped at
point Z because the enzyme
is denatured
[3]

[Total 5 marks]

Exam Practice Tip

Make sure you learn how substrate concentration, pH and temperature affect enzyme activity — examiners just love asking questions about it. pH and temperature have similar effects — so a graph of temperature against rate of reaction or pH against rate of reaction will be the same shape. It's a bit different with substrate concentration though.

More on Enzyme Activity

1 The enzyme amylase breaks down starch to sugar.

A student investigated the effect of pH on amylase activity. He followed this method:

1. Put a drop of iodine solution in each well of a spotting tile.
2. Add amylase and buffer solution to a test tube.
3. Add starch solution to the test tube.
4. Take a sample of the test tube mixture every 30 seconds.
   Add the sample to a well on the spotting tile.

Iodine solution is a browny-orange colour. It turns blue-black in the presence of starch. The student recorded the colour of the iodine solution after each sample was added to the spotting tile. The results for pH 4 are shown in **Figure 1**.

Figure 1

Time (s)	Colour
30	Blue-black
60	Blue-black
90	Blue-black
120	Browny-orange
150	Browny-orange

a) At what time point did the student first record that there was no starch left in the mixture?

....
[1]

The student repeated the experiment at different pH values.

b) At pH 6, the reaction took 120 s to complete.
Calculate the rate of reaction at pH 6. Give your answer to 2 significant figures.

$$\frac{1000}{120} =$$

Rate = ...8.33.... s⁻¹
[2]

c) Give **two** variables that the student should control in this experiment.

1. Amylase catalyses the breakdan from staren lu sugar

2. ....
[2]

d) The student wants to improve the accuracy of his results.
Describe **one** way that the experiment could be improved to give more accurate results.

.... the student can detect starch ....
.... using iodine solution ....
[1]

[Total 6 marks]

Diffusion, Osmosis and Active Transport

Warm-Up

The diagram on the right shows two cells. Draw an arrow between the cells to show the direction in which carbon dioxide will diffuse.

carbon dioxide concentration = 0.2%	carbon dioxide concentration = 1.5%

cell

1 Some molecules move by osmosis. (Grade 3-4)

a) In which **one** of these scenarios is osmosis occurring?

[✓] **A** Water is moving from the mouth down into the stomach.

[ ] **B** Sugar is being taken up into the blood from the gut.

[ ] **C** A plant is absorbing water from the soil.

[ ] **D** Oxygen is entering the blood from the lungs.

[1]

b) Use the words in the box to complete the following definition of osmosis:

water	more	less	sugar

Osmosis is the movement of ....water........ molecules across a partially

permeable membrane from a ....less........ concentrated solution

to a ....more........ concentrated solution.

[3]

[Total 4 marks]

2 **Figure 1** shows a plant root hair cell. It is surrounded by mineral ions (NO_3^- and K^+). (Grade 4-5)

Figure 1

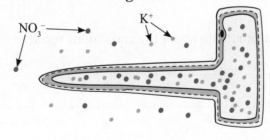

Explain why the root hair cell needs to use active transport to absorb the mineral ions.

........Because it requires energy which........

........is released by respiration........

[Total 2 marks]

Section 1 — Key Concepts in Biology

PRACTICAL

Investigating Osmosis

1 A student did an experiment to see the effect of different sucrose solutions on pieces of potato.

- He cut five equal-sized chips from a raw potato and measured the mass of each chip.
- Each chip was placed in a beaker containing a different concentration of sucrose solution.
- The mass of each chip was measured again after 1 hour. The results are shown in **Figure 1**.

Figure 1

	Beaker				
	1	2	3	4	5
Concentration of sucrose solution (M)	0.1	0.3	0.5	0.7	0.9
% change in mass of potato chip	+9	+2	−3	+19	....

a) The mass of the potato chip in Beaker 5 was 10.0 g before the experiment and 9.3 g afterwards. Calculate the percentage change in mass of the potato chip in Beaker 5.

.... %

[2]

b) Water moved into the potato cylinders in **two** of the beakers. State the numbers of these **two** beakers. Give a reason for your answer.

Beakers: ....

Reason: ....

[2]

c) One of the results in **Figure 1** is anomalous. State the number of the beaker with the anomalous result. Explain your answer.

....

....

[2]

d) Describe what the student should do about the anomalous result.

....

....

[1]

[Total 7 marks]

Exam Practice Tip

As well as being able to interpret any results that you're given, you also need to know how you would go about carrying out this experiment yourself. So learn the method that you would use, including how to calculate the percentage change in mass. As with all experiments, there will be factors that you need to control — such as the size of the potato chips.

Section 1 — Key Concepts in Biology

Mitosis

1   New skin cells can be made by mitosis.

a) Draw straight lines to match the stage of mitosis on the left to its description on the right.

Description

Stage of mitosis

| prophase |

| telophase |

| The chromosomes line up at the centre of the cell. |

| Membranes form around each new set of chromosomes. |

| The membrane around the nucleus breaks down. |

| Each chromosome is split in half. |

[2]

b) Complete the table in **Figure 1** to show which statements apply to new cells produced by mitosis. Tick **two** boxes.

Figure 1

Statement	New cells
The new cells are haploid.	
The new cells are diploid.	✓
The new cells are different to each other.	
The new cells are identical to each other.	✓

[2]

[Total 4 marks]

2   Mitosis is part of the cell cycle.

a) Before mitosis begins, a cell goes through interphase.
Describe what happens during interphase.

Belve mitvu me cell meuw a cop or
is DNA during interphase me DNA is all spread
out in long things

[2]

b) **Figure 2** shows a cell undergoing mitosis.

Name the stage of mitosis that the cell is going through.

Anaphase

[1]

Figure 2

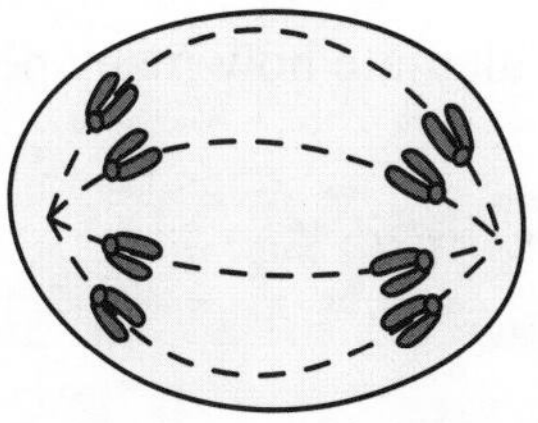

[Total 3 marks]

Cell Division and Growth

1 Animals and plants grow in slightly different ways. *(Grade 3-4)*

a) Cell differentiation is part of both animal and plant growth.
Describe what is meant by cell differentiation.

......Cell differentiation is growth how a.......
......cell changes to become specialised.......
......for a job.......

[1]

b) Apart from cell differentiation, state **two** processes involved in plant growth.

1. .....One is cell elongation.....
2. .....Second is cell division.....

[2]

[Total 3 marks]

2 Percentile charts are used to record and monitor a child's growth. *(Grade 4-5)*

A child's mass was recorded regularly and plotted on the percentile chart shown in **Figure 1**.
The crosses represent the child's mass at different ages.

Figure 1

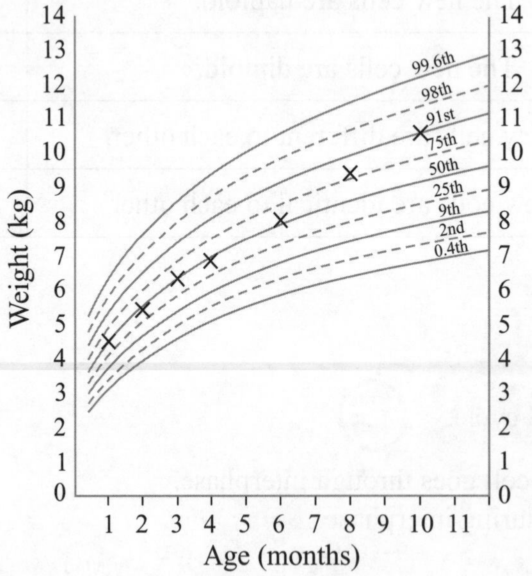

a) At the age of 1 month, what percentile was the child in for his weight?

....

[1]

b) Calculate how many percentiles the child's weight had increased by at the age of 10 months.

.... percentiles
[2]

[Total 3 marks]

Stem Cells

Warm-Up

Circle one word or phrase in bold in each sentence below, so the sentence is correct.

Stem cells are able to **differentiate** / **mutate** to become different types of cells.

Stem cells found in **adults** / **early human embryos** can produce any type of cell.

Plant stem cells can produce **only a small number of cell types** / **any cell type**.

1 Stem cells can be found in plants. *(Grade 3-4)*

Figure 1

a) Name the plant tissue that produces stem cells.

...... Meristems ......
[1]

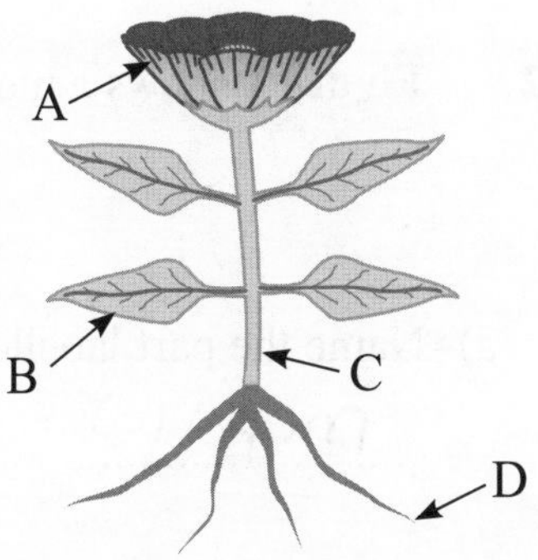

b) **Figure 1** shows a flowering plant.

Which label (**A-D**) shows a site where stem cells are produced?

☐ **A**   ☐ **B**   ☐ **C**   ☐ **D**
[1]

[Total 2 marks]

2 Scientists can use stem cells to grow new cells, which they can then use to test new drugs. *(Grade 4-5)*

a) What are stem cells?

...... They are undifferentiated cells ......
[1]

b) i) Explain **one** reason why scientists may prefer to use embryonic stem cells for research rather than adult stem cells.

...... Scientist may prefer to use embryonic stem cells ......
...... as they are important in the growth ......
...... and development of organisms ......
[2]

ii) Suggest **one** reason why people are against research involving embryonic stem cells.

...... People believe that it should not be used as ......
...... each cell is a human life ......
[1]

c) Scientists are also researching the use of stem cells to cure some diseases.
Suggest **one** risk of using stem cells in medical treatments.

...... They could contain a virus which could be passed on to ......
...... the new person ......
[1]

[Total 5 marks]

The Nervous System

1 The nervous system allows communication between different parts of the body. (Grade 3-4)

Which **one** of the following shows the correct pathway for a nervous response?

☐ **A** sensory neurone — sensory receptor — relay neurone — motor neurone — effector

☐ **B** sensory receptor — sensory neurone — relay neurone — motor neurone — effector

☐ **C** effector — sensory neurone — relay neurone — motor neurone — sensory receptor

☐ **D** sensory receptor — relay neurone — motor neurone — sensory neurone — effector

[Total 1 mark]

2 **Figure 1** shows a motor neurone. (Grade 4-5)

Figure 1

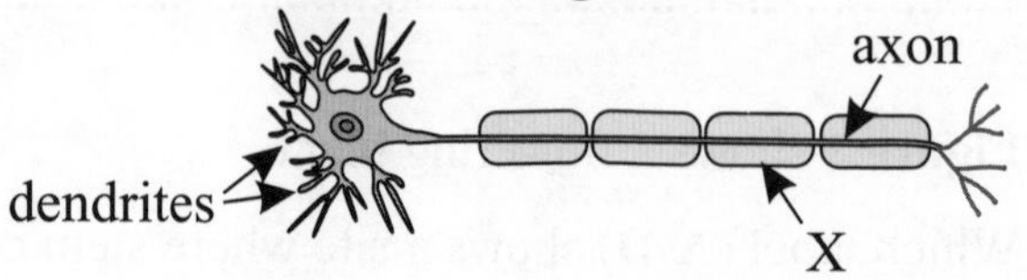

dendrites

axon

X

a) Name the part labelled **X**.

myelin sheath

[1]

b) The cell body of a motor neurone was measured to be 0.09 mm wide.
   Give 0.09 mm as a measurement in μm.

.... μm

[1]

c) Describe how the dendrites and axon help the motor neurone to carry out its function.

Dendrites and axon help me motor neurone carry out it function as mey carry nervous impulses nowards and away the cell body

[2]

d) Explain why a person may not be able to respond to a stimulus if a motor neurone is damaged.

The nervous system is made of neurones so if the nervous are damaged the which allows reaction me stimuls can not respond.

[2]

[Total 6 marks]

Exam Practice Tip

Questions that test your maths skills could crop up anywhere in the exams. Make sure you know how to convert one unit to another. To go from a bigger unit to a smaller unit (for example, from millimetres to micrometres) your calculation should be a <u>multiplication</u>. To go from a smaller unit to a bigger unit, your calculation should be a <u>division</u>.

Synapses and Reflexes

Which of these actions is a reflex?
Circle the correct answer.

Dropping a hot plate.

Writing a letter.

Running to catch a bus.

---

1 Which **one** of the following sentences is correct? (Grade 3-4)

☐ **A** Reflex reactions are rapid and automatic.

☐ **B** Reflex reactions are rapid and under conscious control.

☐ **C** Reflex reactions are slow and automatic.

☐ **D** Reflex reactions are slow and under conscious control.

[Total 1 mark]

---

2 **Figure 1** shows a reflex arc. (Grade 4-5)

Figure 1

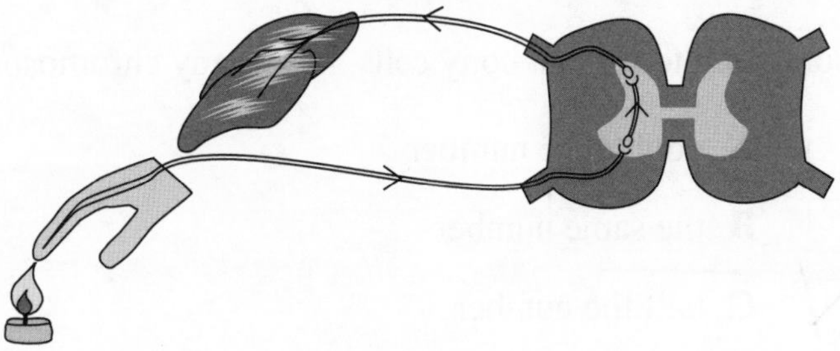

a) State the purpose of the reflex arc shown in **Figure 1**.

...Impulses are sent along a sensory neurone to the CNS

[1]

b)* Describe fully the pathway involved in the reflex arc shown in **Figure 1**.

....

....

....

....

....

....

....

....

....

[6]

[Total 7 marks]

Section 2 — Cells and Control

Section 3 — Genetics

Sexual Reproduction and Meiosis

1 Sexual reproduction involves male and female gametes.

Draw **one** straight line from each type of gamete on the left to its name on the right.

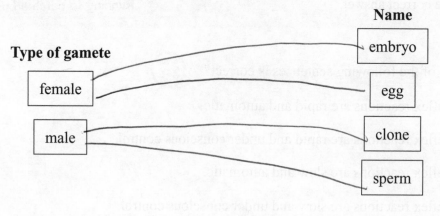

Type of gamete

| female |
| male |

Name

| embryo |
| egg |
| clone |
| sperm |

[Total 2 marks]

2 Gametes are cells produced by meiosis.

a) Compared to normal body cells, how many chromosomes do the cells produced by meiosis have?

☐ **A** double the number

☐ **B** the same number

☑ **C** half the number

☐ **D** triple the number

[1]

b) What does meiosis produce?

☐ **A** two genetically identical daughter cells

☐ **B** four genetically identical daughter cells

☐ **C** two genetically different daughter cells

☑ **D** four genetically different daughter cells

[1]

c) During sexual reproduction, the male gamete fertilises the female gamete.
State the name given to the cell formed from two gametes at fertilisation.

...... The name given is zygote ......

[1]

[Total 3 marks]

Exam Practice Tip

There are two divisions in meiosis. In the first division, one cell splits to give two cells. In the second division, these two cells each split into another two cells. So, you end up with four cells altogether. Each cell gets a different mix of chromosomes — so they're all different. Remember those things, and you'll be off to a good start.

DNA

1 Scientists have studied the human genome. *(Grade 4-5)*

a) What is meant by the term 'genome'?

..... All ov an organism DNA .....

[1]

b) The human genome contains over 20 000 genes.
Explain what is meant by the term 'gene'.

..... A gene is a section of DNA on a chromosone
each gene codes for a particular protein .....

[1]

c) Describe how DNA is stored in the nucleus of eukaryotic cells.

.....

.....

[2]

[Total 4 marks]

2 **Figure 1** shows a section of a DNA double helix. *(Grade 4-5)*

Figure 1

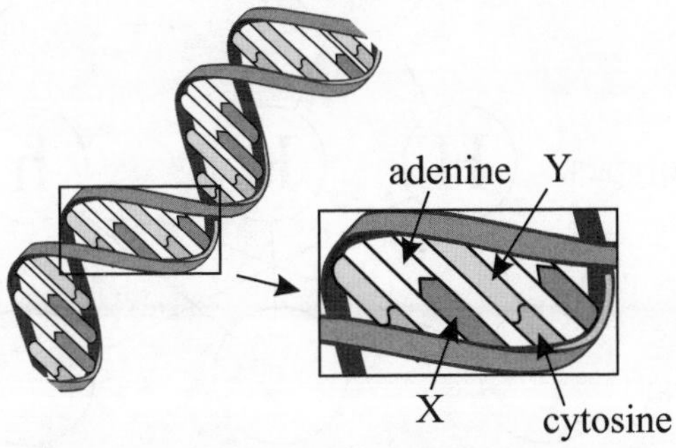

adenine   Y

X   cytosine

a) Name the bases labelled **X** and **Y** on **Figure 1**.

X: ..... label is bases .....

Y: ..... label is strands .....

[2]

b) What is meant by the term 'double helix'?

..... Two strands or a dna molecule coiled together .....

[1]

c) DNA is a polymer. Explain what this means.

..... This mean they're made up of lon of
repeating units joined together .....

[1]

[Total 4 marks]

Genetic Diagrams

Use the words and phrases to complete the passage below.
You don't have to use every one.

homozygous   alleles   multiple genes   dominant

Genes exist in different versions called ....

If the two versions are the same, the organism is .... for that gene.

Some characteristics are controlled by a single gene, but most are controlled by

....

1   Hair length in dogs is controlled by two alleles. Short hair is caused by the dominant allele, 'H'. Long hair is caused by the recessive allele, 'h'.

Figure 1 shows a genetic diagram of a cross between a short-haired and a long-haired dog. The offspring's genotypes are not shown.

Figure 1

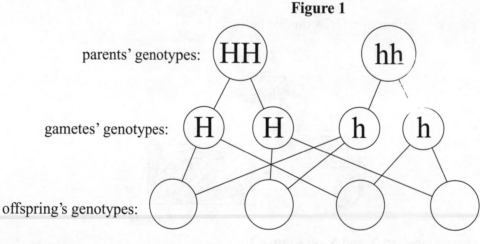

parents' genotypes: HH   hh

gametes' genotypes: H H h h

offspring's genotypes:

a) Circle the long-haired parent in **Figure 1**.

[1]

b) All the offspring have the same genotype.
What is the offspring's genotype? Tick **one** box.

   A Hh   **B** HH   **C** h   **D** hh

[1]

c) What phenotype do the offspring have?

....

[1]

[Total 3 marks]

More Genetic Diagrams

1   **Figure 1** is an incomplete genetic diagram.
    It shows how the biological sex of offspring is determined.

Figure 1

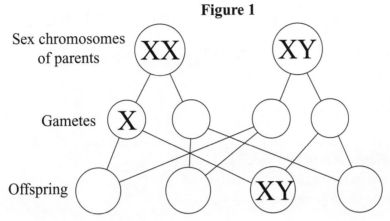

a) Circle the male parent in **Figure 1**.

[1]

b) Fill in the sex chromosomes of the gametes produced by each parent in **Figure 1**.

[1]

c) Complete **Figure 1** to show the combination of sex chromosomes in the offspring.

[1]

d) What is the ratio of male to female offspring in the cross in **Figure 1**?

....

[1]

[Total 4 marks]

2   Cystic fibrosis is an inherited disorder.
    The allele which causes cystic fibrosis is a recessive allele, 'f'.
    'F' represents the dominant allele.

    Figure 2 is an incomplete Punnett square.
    It shows the possible inheritance of cystic fibrosis from one couple.

Figure 2

	F	F
F	FF	Ff
F	FF	

a) Complete the Punnett square to show:
    • the missing gametes' genotypes,   • the missing offspring's genotype.

[2]

b) What proportion of the possible offspring are heterozygous?

....

[1]

c) What proportion of the possible offspring have cystic fibrosis?

....

[1]

[Total 4 marks]

Section 3 — Genetics

Variation

1   Variation in organisms can be caused by genetic factors.   Grade 1-3

Give **two** causes of genetic variation.

1. .....The first one is different alleles.....

2. .....The second is during sexual reproduction.....

[Total 2 marks]

2   **Figure 1** shows two plants of different species, **A** and **B**.   Grade 3-4
Both plants were grown in the same controlled
environmental conditions in a greenhouse.

Figure 1

A   B

Give **one** example of a difference between plants **A** and **B** which is likely to be due to
genetic variation.

.....The environment A grew on a sunny.....
area causing it to be luscious and [Total 1 mark]
green where as B wasn't

3   Helen and Stephanie are identical twins. This means they have identical DNA.   Grade 4-5

Helen weighs 7 kg more than Stephanie.
Explain what type of variation is causing the difference in weight between Helen and Stephanie.

.....It is environmental variation on.....
phenoype they are also called
acquired characteristics
[Total 2 marks]

Exam Practice Tip

Remember, variation is usually caused by a mixture of both environmental and genetic factors, not just one or the other.
In the exam, you might get an example of variation that you've never heard of before. Don't worry if you do, all the
information you need to answer the question will be there. Just apply your knowledge.

Mutations and The Human Genome Project

1   Mutations can lead to variation in an organism.   (Grade 1-3)

a) What is a mutation?

    ☐   **A**   Damage to an organism's cells.

    ☐   **B**   A change to an organism's phenotype.

    ☑   **C**   A change in the order of bases in an organism's DNA.

    ☐   **D**   All of an organism's genes.

[1]

b) Use words from the box to complete the sentences below.

a small	a large	no

A single mutation usually has ......*a small*...... effect on an organism's phenotype.

Very rarely, a single mutation will have ......*a large*...... effect on an

organism's phenotype.

[2]

[Total 3 marks]

2*   Scientists are trying to work out what all of the genes in the human genome do, using the findings of the Human Genome Project.   (Grade 4-5)

Discuss how knowing the functions of all of the genes in the human genome could have benefits in medicine.

It may make it easier to predict and prevent diseases in a person. Certain genes may react differently to different drug however it the doctor knew what type of gene the patient had they would be able to prescribe the suitable drug needed for the patient

[Total 6 marks]

Natural Selection and Evidence for Evolution

Circle the name of the scientist who developed the theory of evolution by natural selection.

Richard Leakey   Carl Linneaus   Carl Woese   Charles Darwin

1 In a population of mice, 70% are grey and 30% are brown. Fur colour is an inherited characteristic.

Grade 3-4

a) Explain why the mice show differences in fur colour.

....

[1]

Selection pressures are things that affect an organism's chance of surviving.

b) State **two** selection pressures that the mice might face.

1. ....

2. ....

[2]

[Total 3 marks]

2 *S. aureus* is a bacterium. It can cause serious illness in some people. Some strains of *S. aureus* have developed resistance to the antibiotic meticillin. These strains are known as MRSA.

Grade 4-5

a) **Figure 1** shows **four** different stages that led to *S. aureus* becoming resistant to meticillin. Put the stages in order by writing the correct number (**1, 2, 3** or **4**) in the space provided.

Figure 1

Number of stage	Stage
....	The gene for meticillin resistance became more common in the population. Eventually most of the population of *S. aureus* had resistance.
....	Individual bacteria with the genes for meticillin resistance were more likely to survive and reproduce in a host being treated with meticillin.
....	The population of *S. aureus* showed variation. A few individuals were resistant to meticillin.
....	The gene for meticillin resistance was passed on to lots of offspring. These offspring survived and reproduced.

[2]

b) Explain why the spread of antibiotic-resistant bacteria is an example of evolution by natural selection.

....

....

[2]

[Total 4 marks]

Fossil Evidence for Human Evolution

Warm-Up

The sentences below are about 'Ardi' — a fossil of a human ancestor.
Circle **one** word in bold in each sentence below, so the sentences are correct.

Ardi's features are a mixture of those found in humans and **apes** / **wolves**.

The structure of her **hands** / **legs** suggests that she walked upright like a human.

But the structure of her **brain** / **feet** suggests she climbed trees.

Ardi provides evidence for human **evolution** / **reproduction**.

---

1   'Turkana Boy', 'Lucy' and 'Ardi' are all fossils of human ancestors.

a) **Figure 1** shows a timeline.
Add an arrow to the timeline to show when the fossil 'Lucy' lived.

Figure 1

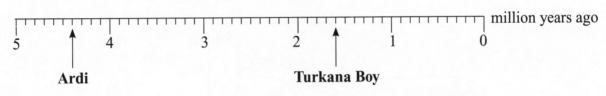

[1]

b) Calculate how many years separated the lives of 'Ardi' and 'Turkana Boy'.

.... million years
[1]
[Total 2 marks]

---

2   'Turkana Boy' is a fossil of the species *Homo erectus*.

a) Which scientist discovered 'Turkana Boy'?

☐ **A** Carl Woese   ☐ **C** Alfred Russel Wallace

☐ **B** Charles Darwin   ☐ **D** Richard Leakey

[1]

b) Give **two** features of the 'Turkana Boy' skeleton, which suggest that his species was more human-like than the species of 'Ardi' or 'Lucy'.

1. ....

2. ....
[2]
[Total 3 marks]

3 A scientist is comparing a number of skeletons of human ancestors.
He estimates their brain sizes using their skull remains.
His results are shown in **Figure 2**.

Figure 2

Specimen	1	2	3
Brain size (cm³)	950	325	457

State and explain which specimen is likely to have lived longest ago.

....

....

[Total 2 marks]

4 Human ancestors began using stone tools around 2.6 million years ago.
Being able to date stone tools allows scientists to see how they developed over time.

Figure 3

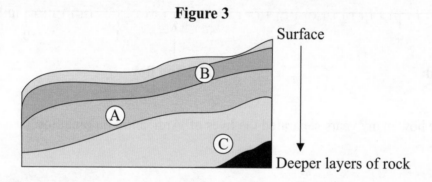

Figure 3 shows the distribution of three stone tools (**A-C**) across the layers of rock at a fossil site.

a) The tool found at site **C** is the oldest.
Explain how you know that this is the case, using evidence from **Figure 3**.

....

....

[2]

b) State and explain which of the tools, **A**, **B**, or **C**, is likely to be the most complex.

....

....

....

[3]

[Total 5 marks]

Classification

Circle the correct word on the right to show whether each statement below is **true** or **false**.

Fish are members of the animal kingdom.	True / False
Bacteria are members of the plant kingdom.	True / False
Mushrooms are members of the fungi kingdom.	True / False

1 Classification involves arranging living organisms into groups. In one system of classification, organisms are first arranged into five groups called kingdoms. *(Grade 3-4)*

a) State the five kingdoms in this classification system.

....

[1]

b) What is the correct order of the following groups in the five kingdom classification system, from biggest to smallest?

☐ **A** phylum, kingdom, class, order, family, species, genus

☐ **B** species, genus, phylum, family, kingdom, order, class

☐ **C** kingdom, genus, phylum, class, order, species, family

☐ **D** kingdom, phylum, class, order, family, genus, species

[1]

[Total 2 marks]

2 Nowadays, the three domain classification system is widely used to classify organisms. One of the domains is Eukarya. *(Grade 4-5)*

a) Name the other **two** domains in the three domain system.

1. ....

2. ....

[2]

b) To create the two domains you named in part **a)**, it was decided that the prokaryote kingdom should be split in two. Explain why this was decided.

....

....

[2]

[Total 4 marks]

Selective Breeding

1 Selective breeding is used in several different industries. (Grade 3-4)

a) What is selective breeding?

.... Is when humann chuse which plants or animals
are going to breed

[1]

b) **Figure 1** shows four wheat plants (**A-D**). Each plant has different characteristics.

Figure 1

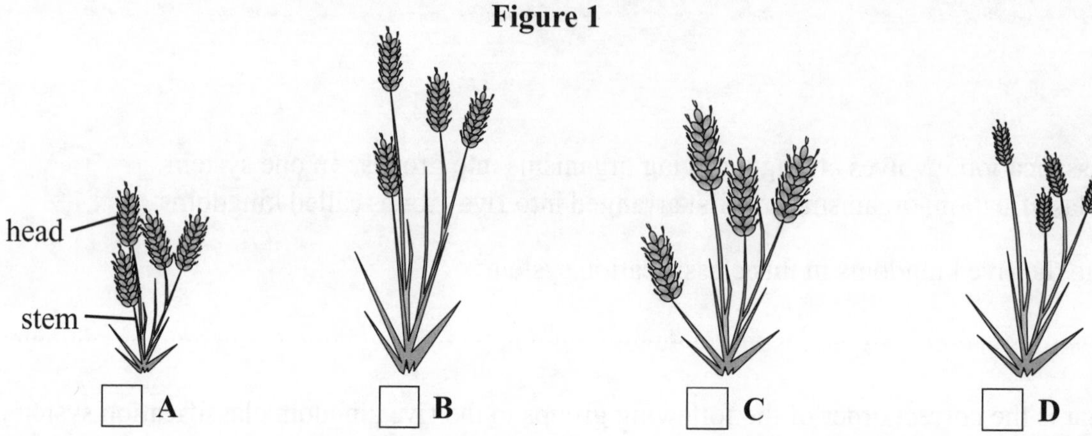

head —
stem —

☐ **A**   ☐ **B**   ☐ **C**   ☐ **D**

Which two plants should be bred together to get a wheat plant with a tall stem and a large head?
Tick **two** boxes.

[1]

c) State **two** problems that can be caused by selective breeding.

1. .. It reduces the number of diffrent allele in a population
2. .. there can also be a serious problem if a
new an appears

[2]

[Total 4 marks]

2 Selective breeding can be used to produce farm animals with certain characteristics. (Grade 4-5)

Describe the process used in selective breeding.

.... the process of selective breeding is from your
existing stock select the ones with the feature you after.
Breed them with each other then select the best
of the offspring and breed them together. Continue this
process over generations and eventually the
offspring will have the feature you want

[Total 3 marks]

Exam Practice Tip

Make sure you understand how selective breeding works, as it could come up in the exam. You could be asked to describe the process of selective breeding in a context that you haven't come across before. You don't need to worry though — as long as you know what the basic process is, you can apply it to any example that comes up.

Section 4 — Natural Selection and Genetic Modification   ☐   ☐   ☺ ☐

Genetic Engineering

1   Crop plants can be genetically engineered to be resistant to herbicides.   (Grade 3-4)

a)   Describe what is meant by genetic engineering.

........Organism.....mat.....have.....had.....a.....new.....gene........

........imened........

[2]

b)   What is the benefit of genetically engineering crop plants to be resistant to herbicides?
Tick **one** box.

☐   **A**   It makes the crop healthier.

☐   **B**   It makes the crop cheaper.

☐   **C**   It can increase crop yield.

☐   **D**   It reduces damage to the crop from pests.

[1]

[Total 3 marks]

2   Some people have concerns about the use of genetic engineering.   (Grade 4-5)

a)   Suggest **one** concern that someone may have about the use of genetic engineering in animals.

....Some.....genetically.....modified.....animals.....also.....suffer.....from.....health....

....problem.....later.....in.....life....
[1]

b)   Suggest **one** concern that someone may have about the use of genetic engineering in crops.

....That.....GM.....crops.....might.....have.....a.....negative.....effect.....on.....food....

....chain.....or.....me.....human.....health....
[1]

[Total 2 marks]

3   A team of scientists are investigating the number of wildflowers in two meadows.
One meadow is next to a field containing a GM crop. The other meadow is next to a field
containing a non-GM crop. The scientists compare their results for the two meadows.   (Grade 4-5)

a)   Suggest why the scientists are carrying out this investigation.

....The.....Scientist.....are.....carry.....out.....his.....investigation....

....to.....compare.....and.....see.....the.....bad.....or.....ask....
[1]

b)   Suggest **one** thing the scientists could do to make their results more valid.

....They.....Crops.....can.....be.....GM'd.....to.....be.....resistant.....to.....herbicides....
[1]

[Total 2 marks]

☹ ☐   ☺ ☐   ☺ ☐   **Section 4 — Natural Selection and Genetic Modification**

Health and Disease

Write the type of pathogen that causes each of the diseases below, using the words on the right. You may use a word more than once, or not at all.

Chalara ash dieback ...... *protist* ......

Tuberculosis ...... *bacterium* ......

Malaria ...... *protist* ......

Cholera ...... *fungus* ......

protist

virus

fungus

bacterium

1 The World Health Organisation (WHO) researches communicable and non-communicable diseases worldwide. *Grade 4-5*

a) Give the WHO's definition of health.

Health is a state of complete physical mental and social well being and not merely the absence of disease or infimity

[2]

b) Describe the difference between a communicable and a non-communicable disease.

The difference is that communicable means contagious whereas non communicable means non contagious

[1]

[Total 3 marks]

2 Tuberculosis is caused by a pathogen. *Grade 4-5*

a) Describe how the pathogen that causes tuberculosis is spread between individuals.

Through the air when infected individuals cough or sneeze

[1]

b) Give **one** effect of tuberculosis on the human body.

lung damage

[1]

c) Describe **one** way in which the spread of the pathogen that causes tuberculosis may be reduced.

....

....

[1]

[Total 3 marks]

STIs

1 Chlamydia is a disease which may result in infertility. *(Grade 3-4)*

a) What type of pathogen causes Chlamydia?

- [ ] **A** protist
- [x] **B** bacterium
- [ ] **C** virus
- [ ] **D** fungus

[1]

b) State how Chlamydia is most commonly transmitted between individuals.

During sexual contact

[1]

Screening individuals for Chlamydia can help to detect the disease.
This can help to reduce the spread of the disease.

c) Suggest why screening can be necessary to detect the disease in some individuals.

In order for them to be treated for the infection

[1]

d) Apart from screening, give **one** additional method for preventing the spread of Chlamydia.

Using protection during sexual activity

[1]

[Total 4 marks]

2 A virus called HIV causes a disease known as AIDS. *(Grade 4-5)*
A person with AIDS has a very weak immune system.

a) Explain why individuals with AIDS are more likely to get other communicable diseases.

As aids reacts to a virus causes a very weak immune system making them more likely to catch communicable diseases

[1]

b) A drug-user shares a needle with another drug-user, who is infected with HIV.
Explain why the first drug-user is at risk from becoming infected with HIV.

As HIV kills white blood cells which are apart of the bodys immune system which helps them fight diseases

[2]

[Total 3 marks]

Section 5 — Health, Disease & the Development of Medicines

Fighting Disease

1 White blood cells are involved in fighting pathogens in the body.

Complete the sentences below. Use words from the box.

lymphocytes	antitoxins	antibodies	antigens	one type	many types

White blood cells called ....Lymphocytes.... produce proteins that lock

onto .... on the surface of pathogens.

The proteins produced by white blood cells are called ....

They will each target .... of pathogen.

[Total 4 marks]

2* The human body has several physical and chemical barriers against the entry of pathogens. Explain how these barriers reduce the number of pathogens entering the body.

Physical The human body has several an physical and chemical barriers against me entry of pathogens a physical barrier is ur skin which stops pathogens getting inside you and it it gets damaged your blood form sticky clots which seal cuts and keep pathogens out

[Total 6 marks]

Exam Practice Tip

Don't panic when you get to a 6 mark question in the exams. Read the question through carefully, then stop and think before you answer. First work out what the question is asking you to write about. Then write down the points you want to make, in an order that makes sense. Make sure you make enough points to get yourself as many marks as possible.

Memory Lymphocytes and Immunisation

Why are people immunised? Underline the correct answer.

To help them get better if they are already ill.

To stop them getting ill in the future.

To get rid of their symptoms.

1 Children are often immunised against measles.   Grade 3-4

a) Which of the following is usually injected into the body during immunisation?

☑ **A** antibiotics

☐ **B** antibodies

☐ **C** dead or inactive pathogens

☐ **D** active pathogens

[1]

b) How should a child's body respond to an immunisation?

know their immune system can quickly respond quickly
to a second infection

[1]

[Total 2 marks]

2 Two children become infected with the measles pathogen.
One child has been immunised against measles and the other has not.   Grade 4-5

Figure 1 shows how the concentration of the measles antibody in each child's bloodstream changes after infection with the measles pathogen.

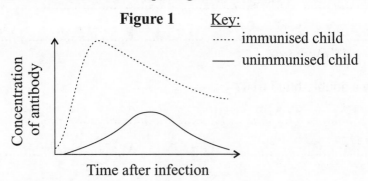

Figure 1   Key:
...... immunised child
——— unimmunised child

Concentration of antibody

Time after infection

Using **Figure 1**, describe how antibody production differs between the immunised child and the unimmunised child.

The pathogens have antigens so your
body makes antibodies to destroy
them

[Total 2 marks]

Antibiotics and Other Medicines

1 What type of diseases can antibiotics be used to treat? **Grade 1-3**

☐ **A** non-communicable diseases   ☐ **C** viral infections

☐ **B** genetic diseases   ☑ **D** bacterial infections

[Total 1 mark]

2 New drugs have to undergo preclinical and clinical testing before they can be used. **Grade 4-5**

a) Which of the following is preclinical testing carried out on?

☐ **A** healthy human volunteers   ☐ **C** patients in a hospital

☐ **B** human cells, tissues and dead animals   ☑ **D** human cells, tissues and live animals

[1]

b) During preclinical testing, scientists test a drug to find out whether it works.
Give **two** more things that the drug is tested for during preclinical testing.

1. How toxic (harmful) it is

2. The dose at which it works best

[2]

During clinical testing, patients are split into two groups.
One group is given the drug. Another group is given a placebo.

c) What is a placebo?

A substance that like the drug being tested but doesn't do anything

[1]

d) Explain why some patients are given the drug and others are given a placebo.

The doctors compare the two groups of patients to see if the drug makes a real difference

[2]

e) What is meant by a double-blind trial?

Neither the patient or the doctor knows whos taking the drug and whos taken the placebo

[1]

[Total 7 marks]

Exam Practice Tip

There's a lot going on when it comes to drug development. The best way to learn what's going on is to write out each step of the process in order, in as much detail as you can. Keep going over it till it sticks. In the exam, you could be asked a question about the development of a particular drug — then it's just a case of applying what you know.

Section 5 — Health, Disease & the Development of Medicines

Non-Communicable Diseases

1 Non-communicable diseases are not spread by pathogens. Instead, they are associated with risk factors.

(Grade 1-3)

Which of the following is the definition of a risk factor for a disease?

☐ **A** A risk factor is something that always causes a disease.

☐ **B** A risk factor is something that an individual is not aware of.

☑ **C** A risk factor is something that increases the likelihood of getting a disease.

☐ **D** A risk factor is part of an individual's lifestyle that they cannot change.

[Total 1 mark]

2 Risk factors for non-communicable diseases include lifestyle factors such as drinking alcohol or smoking.

(Grade 3-4)

a) Give **two** lifestyle factors which increase the risk of obesity.

1. Having a ~~dry~~ diet high in fat and sugar
2. ~~Sett~~ So is not getting enough exercise

[2]

b) Describe how drinking too much alcohol can cause liver disease.

Too much alchol increases the risk of liver disease for example cirhosis who is because the liver breaks down alchol and some of the products can damage liver tissue *[1]*

c) Give **one** disease which is associated with smoking.

Cardiovascular disease

[1]

[Total 4 marks]

3 Non-communicable diseases can be very expensive at a national level.

(Grade 4-5)

Suggest **one** reason why non-communicable diseases can be expensive for a country.

People with non communicable disease may not be able to work and the country loses money and it also cost a lot of money to treat people who have non ~~comma~~ communicable disease *[Total 1 mark]*

Exam Practice Tip

Scientists find risk factors by looking for correlations in data. Many risk factors don't directly cause a disease, but they do make it more likely. A person is even more likely to get a disease if they have several risk factors for it.

 Section 5 — Health, Disease & the Development of Medicines

Measures of Obesity

1 **Figure 1** shows the weight descriptions for a range of BMI values.
Figure 2 shows the BMI values for five patients in a hospital.

Figure 1

Body Mass Index	Weight Description
below 18.5	underweight
18.5 - 24.9	normal
25 - 29.9	overweight
30 - 40	moderately obese
above 40	severely obese

Figure 2

Patient	Sex	BMI
A	Female	16.5
B	Male	26.1
C	Female	30.3
D	Female	30.5
E	Male	20.1

a) Using **Figure 1**, give **two** patients in **Figure 2** who are obese.

....
[1]

b) How many patients in total have a healthy BMI?

....
[1]

[Total 2 marks]

2 A woman has a height of 170 cm and a mass of 73.5 kg.
Her waist circumference is 91 cm and her hip circumference is 84 cm.

a) Calculate the woman's BMI. Give your answer to 3 significant figures.
Use the equation:
$$BMI = \frac{mass\ (kg)}{(height\ (m))^2}$$

BMI = ...kg m^{-2}
[2]

b) Calculate the woman's waist-to-hip ratio. Give your answer to 2 significant figures.
Use the equation:
$$waist\text{-}to\text{-}hip\ ratio = \frac{waist\ circumference}{hip\ circumference}$$

waist-to-hip ratio = ...
[1]

[Total 3 marks]

Section 5 — Health, Disease & the Development of Medicines

Treatments for Cardiovascular Disease

Warm-Up

Fill in the gaps to complete the following sentence. Choose **two** of the words below.

lungs   blood vessels   heart   legs

Cardiovascular diseases are diseases of the ....

and the ....

1   Statins are drugs that can be used to prevent cardiovascular diseases.   *Grade 3-4*

a) What do statins do?

☑ **A** They lower the blood cholesterol level.

☐ **B** They increase the blood cholesterol level.

☐ **C** They remove all cholesterol from the blood.

☐ **D** They help with weight loss.

[1]

b) Give **one** other type of medication which may be used to help prevent cardiovascular disease.

Anticoagulants - Make blood clots less likely to form

[1]

[Total 2 marks]

2   Surgery can be used to treat cardiovascular disease.   *Grade 4-5*

a) Explain how **one** type of surgical procedure can be used to treat cardiovascular disease.

A heart transplant me whole heart is replaced with a donor heart

[2]

b) Give **one** risk of using surgery to treat cardiovascular disease.

Theres a risk a person might get an infection or lose clot or blood

[1]

[Total 3 marks]

     Section 5 — Health, Disease & the Development of Medicines

Photosynthesis

1   Plants use photosynthesis to make glucose.   (Grade 3-4)

a)   Name **one** other type of organism, apart from plants, which uses photosynthesis to make glucose.

....

[1]

b)   Complete the following word equation for photosynthesis.

.... + water → glucose + ...

[2]

c)   Photosynthesis is an endothermic reaction. What is meant by an endothermic reaction?

☐   **A**   Energy is taken in during the reaction.

☐   **B**   Energy is transferred to the environment during the reaction.

☐   **C**   Energy is made during the reaction.

☐   **D**   Energy is broken down during the reaction.

[1]

[Total 4 marks]

PRACTICAL

2   A student did an experiment to see how the rate of photosynthesis is affected by light intensity. She measured the volume of oxygen produced by pondweed at different intensities of light. **Figure 1** shows her results.   (Grade 4-5)

Figure 1

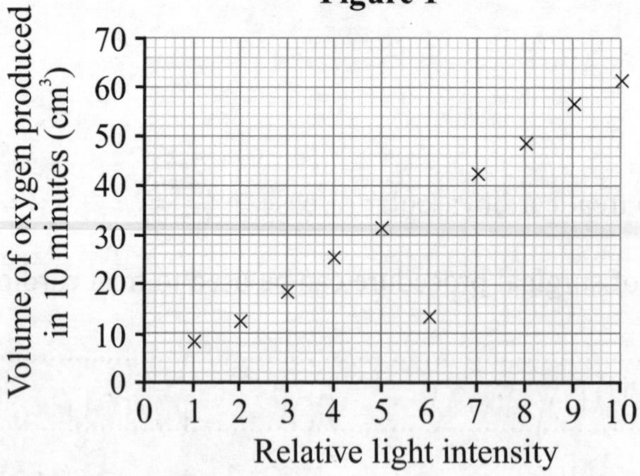

Volume of oxygen produced in 10 minutes (cm³) vs Relative light intensity

a)   One of the student's results is anomalous.
At which relative light intensity is the result anomalous?

Relative light intensity = ...

[1]

b)   Describe what the student's results show about the relationship between light intensity and rate of photosynthesis.

....

[1]

[Total 2 marks]

 ☐   ☐   ☐

Transport in Plants

The diagrams show a phloem tube and a xylem tube.
In the spaces below, write down which one is the phloem tube and which one is the xylem tube.

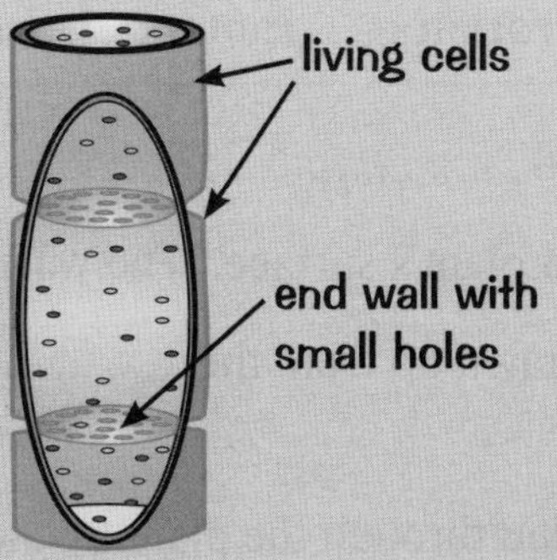

living cells

end wall with small holes

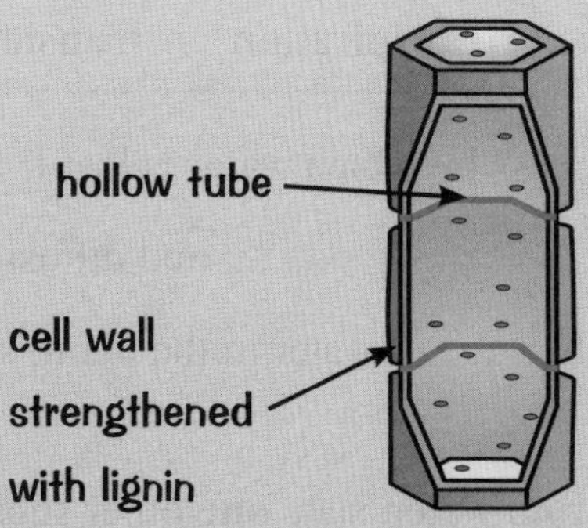

hollow tube

cell wall strengthened with lignin

A: ....

B: ....

1 Phloem and xylem tubes transport substances through a plant. **Grade 3-4**

a) i) Name **one** molecule transported via the phloem.

....

[1]

ii) Name **two** substances transported via the xylem.

1. .... 2. ....

[2]

b) Which of the following statements about transport via the phloem is correct?

☐ **A** It only occurs in the leaves. ☐ **C** It uses energy.

☐ **B** It is called transpiration. ☐ **D** It only moves substances upwards from the roots.

[1]

[Total 4 marks]

2 **Figure 1** shows a diagram of a root hair cell. **Grade 4-5**

Figure 1

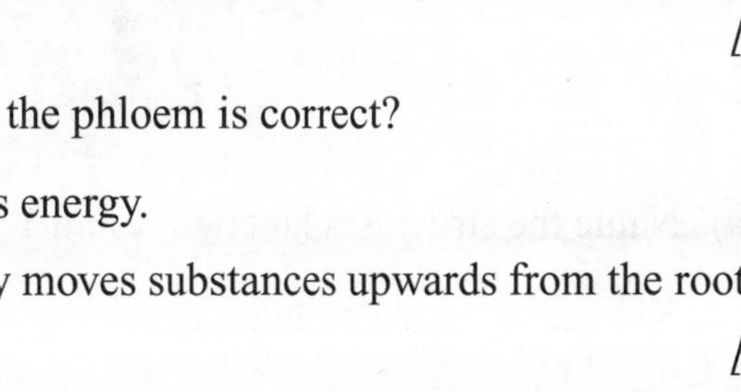

Roots have many individual root hair cells on their surface.
Explain how this helps roots to carry out their function.

....

....

[Total 2 marks]

Section 6 — Plant Structures and Their Functions

Transpiration and Stomata

1   Water moves through plants in a constant stream.

a) Use words from the box to complete the sentences below.
You don't need to use all the words, but each word can only be used once.

> transpiration   translocation   evaporation   roots   leaves

The process by which water is lost from a plant is called .... It is caused by

the .... and diffusion of water from a plant's surface. The water loss creates a

slight shortage of water in the plant, so more water is drawn up from the ....

[3]

b) Apart from water, state **one** other substance that is carried through the plant by the
transpiration stream.

....

[1]

[Total 4 marks]

2   **Figure 1** shows what the surface of a leaf looks like under a microscope.

Figure 1

X   Y

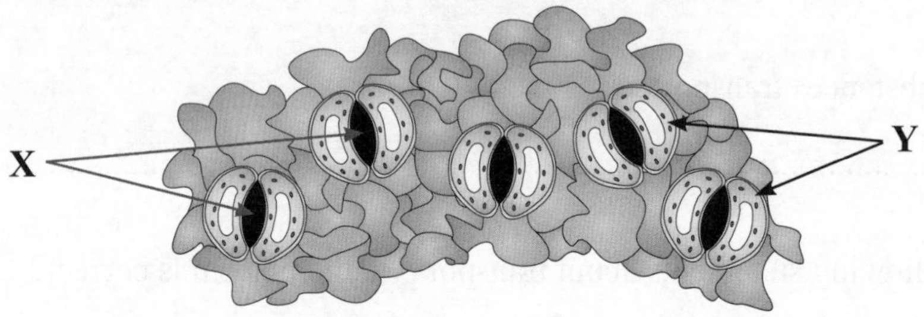

a) Name the structures labelled **X** and **Y** in **Figure 1**.

X ....   Y ....

[2]

b) Explain how the structures labelled **Y** can affect how much water is lost from the plant.

....

....

....

....

[4]

[Total 6 marks]

Exam Practice Tip

The next page is about the factors that affect the rate of transpiration through a plant, so it's a good idea to make sure you understand the basic stuff here first. Think about every stage — how the plant draws up water from the soil, the movement of the water through the whole plant, and then the movement of the water out of the plant into the air.

Transpiration Rate

1 Environmental conditions can affect the rate of transpiration.

Use words from the box to complete the sentences below.

open	closed	faster	slower	more	less

Transpiration is .... in darker conditions.

This is because stomata are .... in the dark.

A warmer temperature leads to a .... transpiration rate because

the water molecules in the leaves have .... energy to move about.

[Total 4 marks]

2 A group of students were investigating the effect of air flow on the rate of transpiration.
To do so, they measured the water uptake of a plant in still and moving air.
The rate of water uptake is assumed to be equal to the transpiration rate.

Figure 1 shows the students' results.

Figure 1

	Repeat	1	2	3	4	5	Mean
Water uptake in 30 minutes (cm³)	Still Air	1.2	1.2	1.0	0.8	1.1	1.1
	Moving Air	2.0	1.8	2.3	1.9	1.7	**X**

a) Calculate the value of **X** in **Figure 1**.
   Give your answer to 2 significant figures.

   X = ... cm³
   [2]

b) Describe the relationship between air flow around the plant and transpiration rate.

   ....
   [1]

c) Explain the effect of air flow on the rate of transpiration.

   ....

   ....

   ....
   [2]

[Total 5 marks]

Section 6 — Plant Structures and Their Functions

Hormones

1 **Figure 1** shows the positions of some glands in the human body.

Figure 1

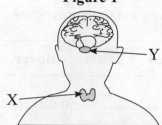

a) Which row of the table identifies the glands labelled **X** and **Y**?

	Gland X	Gland Y
A	pituitary	pancreas
B	thyroid	pituitary
C	thyroid	adrenal
D	adrenal	thyroid

[1]

b) Name the hormone released from the adrenal glands.

....

[1]

[Total 2 marks]

2 Insulin is a hormone. It is secreted by a gland.

a) All the glands in the body are part of the same system. What is the name of this system?

☐ **A** immune system   ☐ **C** digestive system

☐ **B** respiratory system   ☐ **D** endocrine system

[1]

b) What is the name of the gland that secretes insulin?

☐ **A** pituitary   ☐ **B** adrenal   ☐ **C** pancreas   ☐ **D** thyroid

[1]

c) Describe how insulin is transported to its target organ, the liver.

....

[1]

d) State **two** ways in which communication by hormones
differs from communication via the nervous system.

1. ....

2. ....

[2]

[Total 5 marks]

The Menstrual Cycle

1 Oestrogen is a hormone involved in the menstrual cycle. (Grade 3-4)

a) Name the gland that releases oestrogen.

....

[1]

b) Describe how oestrogen affects the uterus lining.

....

[1]

c) The menstrual cycle involves the release of an egg from an ovary.
Name the process by which an egg is released from an ovary.

....

[1]

[Total 3 marks]

2 **Figure 1** shows how two female sex hormones change over the course of the menstrual cycle. (Grade 4-5)

Figure 1

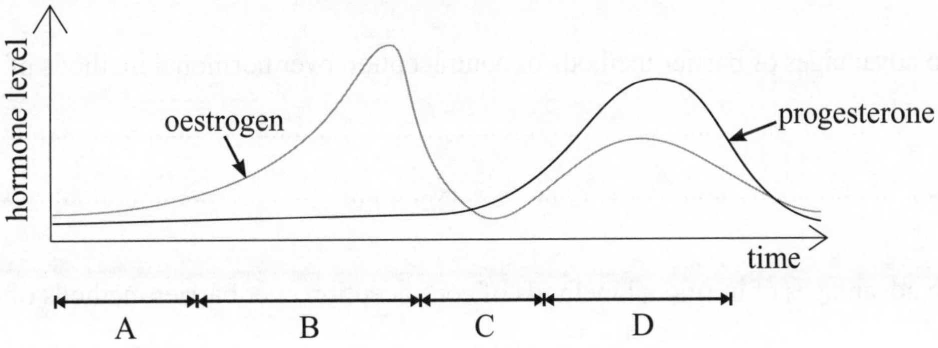

The corpus luteum forms after ovulation. The corpus luteum releases progesterone.

a) State and explain the time period in **Figure 1** (**A**, **B**, **C** or **D**) in which the corpus luteum forms.

....

....

[2]

b) Explain what will happen to the woman when the progesterone level drops.

....

....

....

[3]

[Total 5 marks]

   Section 7 — Animal Coordination, Control and Homeostasis

Contraception

Warm-Up

All of the methods below are forms of contraception. Circle the **two** hormonal methods.

avoiding sexual intercourse   contraceptive injection   contraceptive patch   diaphragm

1 Many people choose barrier methods of contraception to prevent pregnancy. (Grade 4-5)

a) A condom is a form of barrier contraception.
How do condoms prevent pregnancy?

....

[1]

b) With perfect use, for every 600 women who use male condoms as a method of contraception every time they have sex, an average of 12 will become pregnant over the course of a year.

Calculate how effective condoms are, with perfect use, as a percentage.

.... %

[2]

c) Give **two** advantages of barrier methods of contraception over hormonal methods of contraception.

1. ....

2. ....

[2]

d) Give **two** advantages of hormonal methods of contraception over barrier methods of contraception.

1. ....

2. ....

[2]
[Total 7 marks]

2 Some methods of contraception use hormones to control the fertility of a woman. (Grade 4-5)

State **one** hormone used in hormonal contraception and explain how it prevents women from getting pregnant.

....

....

....

[Total 2 marks]

Section 7 — Animal Coordination, Control and Homeostasis

Homeostasis — Control of Blood Glucose

Circle the correct word on the right to show whether each statement below is **true** or **false**.

Conditions inside the body need to be kept steady.	true / false
If the level of glucose in the blood is too high, the body will act to reduce it.	true / false
Glycogen is stored in the muscle cells.	true / false

1 Homeostasis is an important process.   (Grade 3-4)

a) What is homeostasis?

☐ **A** Maintaining a constant internal environment in response to external changes only.

☐ **B** Maintaining a constant internal environment in response to internal changes only.

☐ **C** Maintaining a constant internal environment in response to internal and external changes.

☐ **D** Maintaining a constant external environment in response to internal and external changes.

[1]

b) Explain why homeostasis is important.

....

....

[2]

[Total 3 marks]

2 The concentration of glucose in the blood is controlled by hormones.   (Grade 3-4)

a) Which gland in the human body monitors and controls blood glucose concentration?

☐ **A** pancreas   ☐ **B** pituitary gland   ☐ **C** thyroid   ☐ **D** testis

[1]

b) Which hormone is produced when blood glucose concentration becomes too high?

....

[1]

c) Complete the sentences to describe what happens when there is too much glucose in the blood.
Use words from the box.

pancreas	**glycogen**	**insulin**	**liver**

When there is too much glucose in the blood, some of it moves into the ....

The glucose is then changed into .... so it can be stored.

[2]

[Total 4 marks]

☹ ☐   🙂 ☐   😊 ☐   Section 7 — Animal Coordination, Control and Homeostasis

Diabetes

1 Diabetes exists in two different forms, type 1 and type 2. Grade 1-3

a) Which of these describes **type 1** diabetes?

☐ **A** The body produces too little glucose.

☐ **B** The body becomes resistant to its own insulin.

☐ **C** The body produces too much insulin.

☐ **D** The body doesn't make insulin.

[1]

b) How is **type 1** diabetes treated?

....

[1]

[Total 2 marks]

2 A patient visits her health centre because she is concerned she is at risk of developing type 2 diabetes. Grade 4-5

a) The nurse wants to check the patient's BMI.

i) State **two** measurements the nurse needs to take in order to calculate the patient's BMI.

1. ....

2. ....

[2]

ii) Explain why the nurse wants to check the patient's BMI.

....

....

[2]

b) Give **two** treatments that the patient's doctor might recommend if the patient was later diagnosed with type 2 diabetes.

1. ....

2. ....

[2]

[Total 6 marks]

Exam Practice Tip

This stuff links to homeostasis. Diabetes is where a mechanism involved in homeostasis stops working properly. As a result, the blood glucose concentration is able to rise too high. Remember, there are two types of diabetes — so don't get them mixed up in the exam. The two types have different causes and can sometimes be treated in different ways.

Section 7 — Animal Coordination, Control and Homeostasis

 ☐ ☐ ☐

Exchange of Materials

Warm-Up

Place the following organisms in order according to their surface area to volume ratio.
Number the boxes 1 to 3, with 1 being the smallest and 3 being the largest.

☐ Tiger   ☐ Bacterium   ☐ Blue whale

---

1 In order to survive, mammals, like all organisms, must exchange substances with their environment. *Grade 3-4*

a) Give **two** substances that a mammal must transport into its body in order to survive.

....
[2]

b) Give **two** substances that a mammal must get rid of in order to survive.

....
[2]

[Total 4 marks]

---

2 The cube in **Figure 1** represents a small cell. *Grade 4-5*

a) Calculate the volume of the cube.

Figure 1

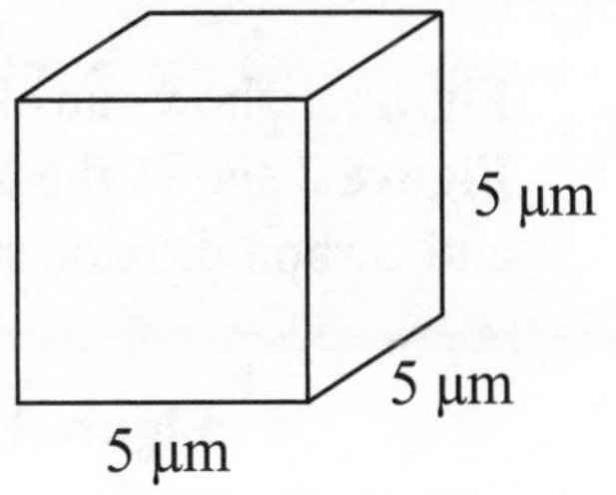

5 µm
5 µm
5 µm

volume = ...µm³
[1]

b) Calculate the surface area of the cube.

surface area = ... µm²
[2]

c) Another cell has a surface area of 24 µm². It has a volume of 8 µm³.
Write its surface area to volume ratio in its simplest form.

surface area to volume ratio = ...
[1]

[Total 4 marks]

 ☐   ☐   ☐

Specialised Exchange Surfaces — the Alveoli

1 Gas exchange in mammals happens in the alveoli.   (Grade 3-4)

a) Describe the movement of the gases that are exchanged in the alveoli.

....

....

[2]

b) By what process do gases move across the membrane of an alveolus?

....

[1]

c) State which feature of the alveoli gives gases a short distance to move.

....

[1]

d) Apart from having a short distance for gases to move, state **one** other feature of the alveoli which allows gas exchange to take place quickly.

....

[1]

[Total 5 marks]

2 **Figure 1** shows an alveolus in the lungs.
Figure 2 shows the relative concentrations of oxygen
and carbon dioxide at positions **X**, **Y** and **Z** in **Figure 1**.   (Grade 4-5)

Figure 1

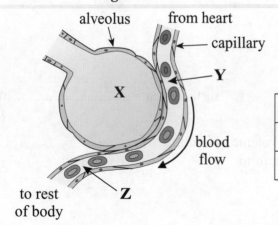

Figure 2

	Oxygen concentration	Carbon dioxide concentration
X	High	Low
Y	Low	....
Z	....	....

Complete **Figure 2** by writing **high** or **low** in the empty cells.

[Total 3 marks]

Circulatory System — Blood

1   The blood has several different parts.

a) **Figure 1** shows three different types of blood cell. Place a tick in each row of the table
to show whether each type of blood cell is a white blood cell or a red blood cell.

Figure 1

		white blood cell	red blood cell
type of blood cell	erythrocyte		
	lymphocyte		
	phagocyte		

[2]

b) The different parts of the blood are carried in a liquid.
What is this liquid called?

☐ **A** urine   ☐ **B** plasma   ☐ **C** cell sap   ☐ **D** bile

[1]

c) Name the part of the blood which is involved in clotting.

....

[1]

[Total 4 marks]

2   **Figure 2** shows the shape of a red blood cell.

Figure 2

View from above   Cut through view

a) What is the function of red blood cells?

....

[1]

b) Describe how a red blood cell's shape helps it to carry out its function.

....

[1]

c) Red blood cells don't have a nucleus.
How does this help them to carry out their function?

....

[1]

[Total 3 marks]

Circulatory System — Blood Vessels

Label each of the following diagrams to show whether each one is a capillary, artery or vein.

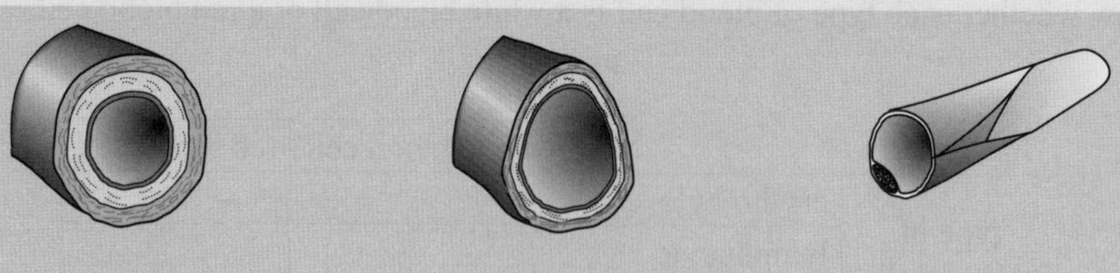

Diagrams not to scale.

A. ....   B. ....   C. ....

1   Different types of blood vessel have different structures.   Grade 3-4

Complete **Figure 1** to show whether each feature is part of a capillary, an artery or a vein. Put a tick in each row.

Figure 1

Feature	Capillary	Artery	Vein
Elastic fibres in blood vessel walls			
Large lumen			
Walls that are one cell thick			
Valves			

[Total 3 marks]

2   The structure of blood vessels is related to their functions.   Grade 4-5

a) Describe the function of capillaries.

....

....

[2]

b) Explain why arteries have a different structure to veins.

....

....

....

[2]

c) Describe the purpose of valves in a blood vessel.

....

[1]

[Total 5 marks]

Circulatory System — Heart

1   **Figure 1** shows a diagram of the heart.

Figure 1

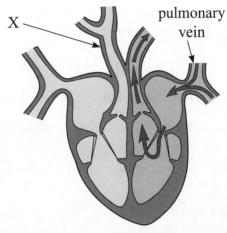

a) What is the part of the heart labelled **X**?

    ☐ **A** vena cava   ☐ **C** aorta

    ☐ **B** pulmonary artery   ☐ **D** left atrium

[1]

The arrows on **Figure 1** show the direction of blood flow through the **left side** of the heart.

b) Draw arrows on **Figure 1** to show the direction of blood flow through the **right side** of the heart.

[1]

[Total 2 marks]

2   The walls of the different chambers of the heart vary in their thickness.

State and explain the difference in thickness between the walls of the left and right ventricles.

....

....

....

[Total 3 marks]

3   Explain why the human circulatory system is described as a 'double circulatory system'.

....

....

....

....

....

[Total 3 marks]

☹ ☐   ☺ ☐   ☺ ☐   **Section 8 — Exchange and Transport in Animals**

Heart Rate Calculations

Warm-Up

Complete the following passage using the words below.

heart rate	stroke volume	cardiac output

A person's .... is the number of times their heart beats in a minute.

.... is the total volume of blood pumped by a ventricle in a minute.

.... is the amount of blood pumped by a ventricle each time it contracts.

1   **Figure 1** shows the heart rate, stroke volume and cardiac output for two athletes at rest.

	Athlete	
Figure 1	1	2
Heart rate (bpm)	57	
Stroke volume (cm³)	90	85
Cardiac output (cm³ min⁻¹)		5525

a) Calculate the **cardiac output** for Athlete **1**.
Use the equation: cardiac output = heart rate × stroke volume

Cardiac output = ... $cm^3 \ min^{-1}$
[1]

b) Calculate the **heart rate** for Athlete **2**.
Use the equation: cardiac output = heart rate × stroke volume

Heart rate = ... bpm
[2]

c) What do the units 'bpm' stand for?

....
[1]

[Total 4 marks]

Exam Practice Tip

Remember, you can just rearrange the equation for finding cardiac output if you need to find heart rate or stroke volume. So don't be put off if the question gives you the equation the wrong way around — you can just switch it yourself.

Section 8 — Exchange and Transport in Animals

Respiration

1   Respiration can be anaerobic or aerobic.

a) **Figure 1** shows four statements about respiration.
Place a tick in each row of the table to show which type of respiration each statement refers to.

Figure 1

Statement	Aerobic respiration	Anaerobic respiration
It transfers more energy.		
It uses oxygen.		
It can produce lactic acid.		

[2]

b) Which type of respiration occurs continuously in plants and animals?

....
[1]

c) Complete the following word equation for respiration involving oxygen.

   glucose + oxygen → carbon dioxide + ...

[1]

[Total 4 marks]

2   Respiration is an important chemical reaction.

a) Complete the following sentences about respiration. Use words from the box.

exothermic	from	endothermic	all	to	some

   Respiration is a reaction carried out by .... living organisms.

   Respiration is an .... reaction.

   It transfers energy .... the environment.

[3]

Figure 2 shows a gull.

Figure 2

b) Give **one** example of how a gull uses the energy transferred by respiration.

....
[1]

[Total 4 marks]

Section 8 — Exchange and Transport in Animals

Investigating Respiration

1   An experiment was set up using a sealed beaker, with a carbon dioxide monitor attached. The set up is shown in **Figure 1**.

Figure 1

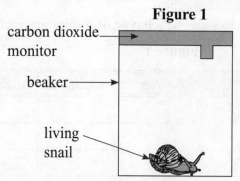

carbon dioxide monitor

beaker

living snail

After two hours, the carbon dioxide concentration in the beaker in **Figure 1** had **increased**.

a) Explain why the carbon dioxide concentration in the beaker increased.

....

[1]

b) Suggest what happened to the level of **oxygen** in the beaker in **Figure 1** after two hours. Explain your answer.

....

....

[2]

c) Suggest **one** ethical consideration that must be taken into account during this experiment.

....

[1]

Figure 2 shows the volume of carbon dioxide in the beaker at 1 hour intervals.

Figure 2

	Time (hours)		
	0	1	2
Volume of carbon dioxide (cm³)	0.2	0.36	0.5

d) Calculate the average rate of respiration of the snail.
Use the equation:

$$\text{average rate of respiration} = \frac{\text{change in } CO_2 \text{ volume}}{\text{time}}$$

rate of respiration = ... cm³ h⁻¹

[2]

[Total 6 marks]

Ecosystems and Interdependence

1 There are different levels of organisation within an ecosystem.

Draw **one** line from each level of organisation on the left to its definition on the right.

definition

level of organisation

all the organisms of
one species in a habitat

community

the place where an organism lives

population

all the organisms of
different species in a habitat

the smallest level in an ecosystem

[Total 2 marks]

2 Organisms within an ecosystem are interdependent.

a) Explain what is meant by the term 'ecosystem'.

....

....

[1]

b) What does it mean if organisms are interdependent?

....

[1]

[Total 2 marks]

3 A species of ant lives in the hollow thorns on a certain species of tree. The ants
feed on the tree's nectar. The ants also protect the tree from harmful bacteria.

The ants and tree have a mutualistic relationship.
Explain why this is an example of a mutualistic relationship.

....

....

....

[Total 2 marks]

Factors Affecting Ecosystems

Warm-Up

Biotic factors are the living factors in an environment. Circle **two** biotic factors below.

water   competition   temperature

pollutants   light   predators

1   Abiotic and biotic factors can affect the distribution of organisms. *(Grade 3-4)*

a) Which **one** of the following statements is correct?

☐ **A** Light intensity and temperature are examples of biotic factors.

☐ **B** Predators and the amount of water are examples of abiotic factors.

☐ **C** Light intensity and the amount of water are examples of abiotic factors.

☐ **D** Predators and light intensity are examples of biotic factors.

[1]

b) Competition over resources can affect the distribution of animal species in an ecosystem.
State **two** resources that animals in an ecosystem might compete over.

1. ....

2. ....

[2]

[Total 3 marks]

2   Foxes are predators. Rabbits are their prey. *(Grade 4-5)*

a) The number of foxes in an ecosystem increases.
State and explain what you think will happen to the number of rabbits in the ecosystem.

....

....

[2]

b) A new disease appears in a rabbit population.
Suggest how this could lead to a decrease in the fox population in the same ecosystem.

....

....

....

[2]

[Total 4 marks]

Investigating Ecosystems

1   **Figure 1** shows a transect line. It is being used to record the distribution of plants in a field.

Figure 1

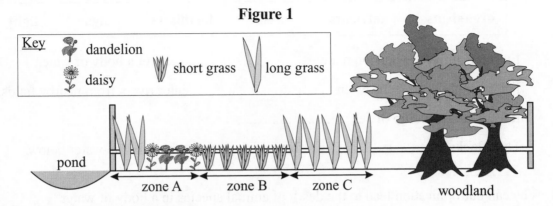

The field is split up into three zones — **A**, **B** and **C**.

a) In **Figure 1**, which zones contained only **one** species of plant?

    ....

    [1]

b) Dandelions grow best in soils which have a high level of moisture.
    Which zone, **A**, **B** or **C**, is most likely to have a high level of moisture?

    ....

    [1]

    [Total 2 marks]

2   A group of students used 1 m² quadrats to compare the population sizes of
    buttercups in two areas of a field. They collected data from three randomly
    placed quadrats in each area. Their results are shown in **Figure 2**.

		Quadrat 1	Quadrat 2	Quadrat 3	Mean
Figure 2	Area 1	15	14	13	14
	Area 2	26	23	18	**X**

a) Calculate the value of **X** in **Figure 2**.
    Give your answer to 2 significant figures.

    X = ...
    [2]

b) **Area 1** has an area of 1750 m².
    Estimate the total number of buttercups in **Area 1**.

    .... buttercups
    [1]

    [Total 3 marks]

Human Impacts on Biodiversity

1   Eutrophication can lead to a reduction in biodiversity.   (Grade 3-4)

   a) Complete the sentences below about eutrophication. Use words from the box.

organisms	nutrients	seeds	fertilisers	algae	light

   Eutrophication is when too many .... enter a body of water.

   For example, it happens when .... enter rivers from nearby fields.

   It leads to a build-up of ....

   This blocks .... from getting to the plants in the water below.

   [4]

   b) Why can eutrophication lead to the death of animal species in a body of water?

   ☐   **A** It reduces the amount of carbon dioxide in the water.

   ☐   **B** It reduces the amount of oxygen in the water.

   ☐   **C** It causes parasites to enter the water.

   ☐   **D** It increases the number of predators in the water.

   [1]

   [Total 5 marks]

2   Fish can be farmed in nets in the ocean.   (Grade 4-5)

   a) Fish food can sometimes escape the nets.
       Explain why this may lead to eutrophication in the water surrounding the nets.

   ....

   ....

   [1]

   b) Fish in fish farms can be infected by parasites.
       Explain how this might affect the biodiversity of areas surrounding the nets.

   ....

   ....

   ....

   [2]

   c) Suggest how fish farmed in nets might affect local fish populations if they escaped into the wild.

   ....

   ....

   ....

   [2]

   [Total 5 marks]

3   Possums are a type of mammal that are indigenous to Australia. They were introduced by humans into New Zealand. *(Grade 3-4)*

Possums compete with native birds in New Zealand for access to shelter.

a) Explain the likely effect that the introduction of possums would have had on the native birds.

....

....

....

[2]

b) Apart from competing with native species, suggest **one** other way that the possums may have negatively affected native wildlife in New Zealand.

....

[1]

[Total 3 marks]

4*   Humans can help to improve biodiversity. Efforts to maintain and improve biodiversity include reforestation programmes and conservation schemes. *(Grade 4-5)*

Describe how reforestation programmes and different types of conservation schemes can help to maintain biodiversity and benefit local populations.

....

....

....

....

....

....

....

....

....

....

[Total 6 marks]

Exam Practice Tip

Unfortunately, humans do lots of things that end up reducing biodiversity (boo, hiss). But remember — there are also lots of ways we can have a positive effect on biodiversity. Make sure you're able to describe a few different methods for protecting or increasing biodiversity. You should also be able to explain how the different methods work.

Section 9 — Ecosystems and Material Cycles

The Carbon Cycle

1 **Figure 1** shows a simplified version of the carbon cycle.

Figure 1

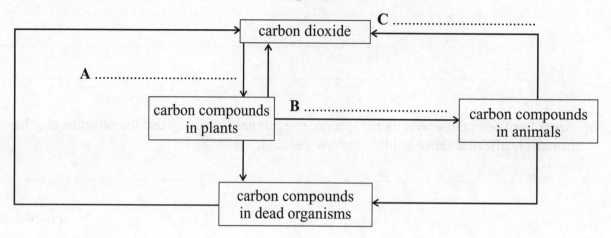

Complete **Figure 1**.
Fill in the labels **A**, **B** and **C** using words from the box.

| decay | respiration | eating | photosynthesis | transpiration |

[Total 3 marks]

2 The carbon cycle describes how carbon moves between organisms and their environment.

a) Explain how microorganisms in the soil release carbon from dead material.

....

....

....
[2]

b) Describe how carbon from the air can become a part of the carbon compounds in a plant.

....

....

....
[2]

[Total 4 marks]

Exam Practice Tip

Make sure you know all of the carbon cycle, not just bits of it. Try sketching out the whole cycle to help you remember it. First write out the different parts, e.g. the air, plants, etc. Then think of the different processes that move carbon around between these parts, e.g. respiration. Draw arrows to show the direction in which these processes move carbon.

The Water Cycle

Find three words that are types of precipitation in the wordsearch below. Circle each of them.

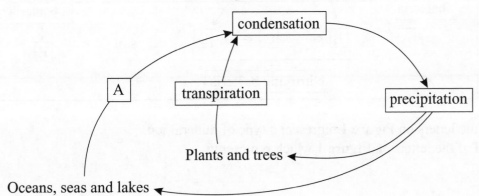

```
g h a v o u p s d
r a i n z x q n k
f d e g t h y o r
s f j h l p e w e
p h a i l w e a a
```

1 Which is a method that can be used to produce drinking water from salt water?

☐ **A** desalination   ☐ **B** denitrification   ☐ **C** contamination   ☐ **D** filtration

[Total 1 mark]

2 **Figure 1** represents the stages in the water cycle.

Figure 1

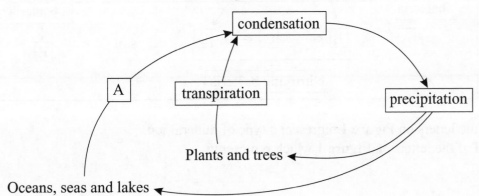

a) Name the process represented by **A** in the diagram.

....
[1]

b) Explain why precipitation is an important stage in the water cycle.

....

....
[1]

[Total 2 marks]

            Section 9 — Ecosystems and Material Cycles

The Nitrogen Cycle

1 Each year, a farmer cuts his crop and removes it from the field. [Grade 3-4]

a) Explain why the amount of nitrogen in the soil in the field will decrease over time.

....

....

[1]

b) State **two** methods the farmer could use to improve the nitrate content of his soil.

1. ....

2. ....

[2]

[Total 3 marks]

2 **Figure 1** shows a simplified diagram of the nitrogen cycle. [Grade 4-5]

Figure 1

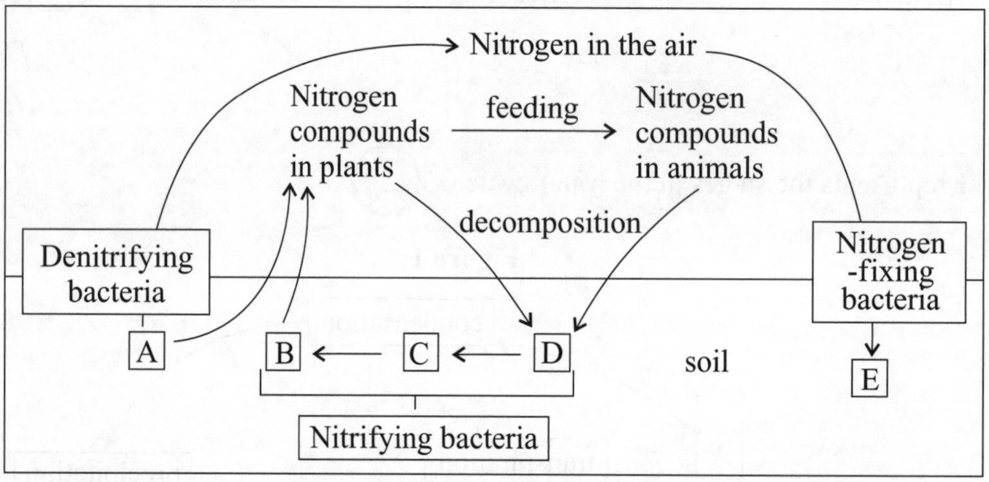

All of the letters on **Figure 1** represent a type of mineral ion.
List **all** of the letters on **Figure 1** which represent:

a) nitrites:

....

[1]

b) ammonia:

....

[2]

c) nitrates:

....

[2]

[Total 5 marks]

Section 9 — Ecosystems and Material Cycles

Chemical Equations

Warm-Up

The word equation for a reaction is shown below:

magnesium + hydrochloric acid → magnesium chloride + hydrogen

For each of the following statements, circle whether the statement is **true** or **false**.

1) Hydrogen is a product in the reaction.   True Or False

2) The equation shows the reaction between chlorine and hydrogen.   True Or False

3) Hydrochloric acid is a reactant.   True Or False

4) The equation shows the reaction between magnesium and hydrochloric acid.   True Or False

1 Look at the following word equation: sodium + water → sodium hydroxide + hydrogen

a) Name the **two** reactants in this reaction.

....

[1]

b) Name the **two** products of this reaction.

....

[1]

[Total 2 marks]

2 **Figure 1** shows the names of some ions and some elements.

a) Place ticks in the correct boxes to show which elements each of these ions contains.

Ion	Element		
	Oxygen	**Hydrogen**	**Nitrogen**
Hydroxide			
Nitrate			
Ammonium			

Figure 1 *[3]*

b) Which elements does a sulfate ion contain? Explain how you can tell this from its name.

Elements: ....

Reason: ....

[2]

[Total 5 marks]

Balancing Equations

1 Draw **one** line from each physical state to match it to the correct state symbol.

Physical state	State symbol

solid   (s)

     (l)

gas   (aq)

liquid   (g)

[Total 3 marks]

2 Sodium (Na) reacts with chlorine gas (Cl_2) to form sodium chloride (NaCl) only.

a) Which of the following equations correctly represents this reaction?
Tick **one** box.

☐ **A** $Na + Cl \rightarrow NaCl$ ☐ **C** $Na_2 + 2Cl \rightarrow 2NaCl$

☐ **B** $Na + Cl_2 \rightarrow NaCl$ ☐ **D** $2Na + Cl_2 \rightarrow 2NaCl$

[1]

b) Sodium also reacts with oxygen (O_2) to form sodium oxide (Na_2O).
Balance the equation for this reaction.

$$............. \ Na + O_2 \rightarrow .... \ Na_2O$$

[2]

[Total 3 marks]

3 Calcium carbonate chips were reacted with hydrochloric acid at room temperature. The products of the reaction were water, a gas and a salt solution.

a) Complete the reaction equation by adding state symbols to describe the reaction.

$$CaCO_{3(s)} + 2HCl_{(aq)} \rightarrow CaCl_2 (...........) + H_2O (...........) + CO_2 (...........)$$

[2]

b) Calcium metal also reacts with hydrochloric acid (HCl)
to form calcium chloride ($CaCl_2$) and hydrogen gas.
Write a balanced equation for this reaction.

....

[2]

[Total 4 marks]

Hazards and Risk

1 Chemicals have hazard symbols on them to show what their dangers are. (Grade 3-4)

Draw **one** line from each hazard below to match it to its description.

Hazard

Oxidising

Highly flammable

Environmental hazard

Description

Harmful to plants or animals and to the environment.

Can cause irritation, reddening or blistering of the skin.

Provides oxygen which allows other materials to burn fiercely.

Catches fire easily.

[Total 3 marks]

2 A student is carrying out an experiment using some hazardous chemicals. One of the chemicals is stored in a flask, marked with the label shown in **Figure 1**. (Grade 4-5)

a) Which of the following hazards are associated with the contents of the flask? Tick **one** box.

☐ **A** oxidising

☐ **B** corrosive

☐ **C** environmental hazard

☐ **D** highly flammable

Figure 1

[1]

b) State **one** safety precaution that the student should take when using the chemical from the flask.

....

[1]

[Total 2 marks]

3 A student is planning an experiment to assess how the rate of a certain reaction changes with concentration. The reaction produces a gas that is toxic. (Grade 4-5)

a) What does it mean if a gas is described as 'toxic'?

....

[1]

b) Describe the safety precautions that the student needs to take to reduce the risk of this experiment.

....

....

[2]

[Total 3 marks]

The History of the Atom

Warm-Up

Use the words to label the different parts of the atom shown below.

shell

electron

nucleus

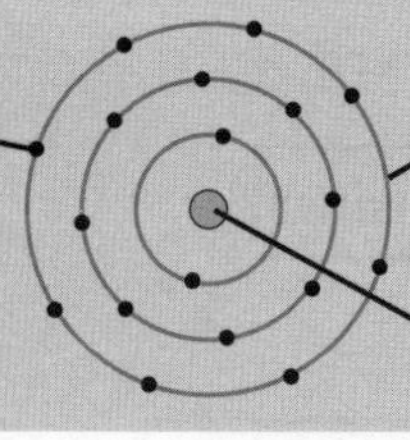

1 Models of the atom have changed over time. **Grade 3-4**

a) Which of the following is the best description of what scientists
thought an atom was like before the electron was discovered?
Tick **one** box.

☐ **A** Solid spheres.   ☐ **B** Formless 'clouds'.   ☐ **C** Flat shapes.   ☐ **D** Packets of energy.

[1]

b) Describe how the charges are arranged in the model shown in **Figure 1**.

....

....

....
[2]

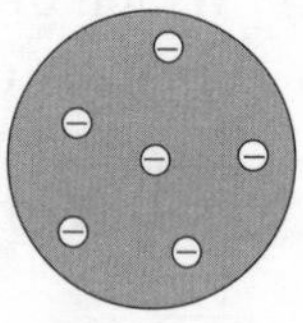

Figure 1

[Total 3 marks]

2 Scientist's understanding of the atom has changed as different particles have been discovered. **Grade 4-5**

a) Scientists discovered a neutral particle inside the nucleus. Give the name of this particle.

....
[1]

b) Part of an atom is positively charged. Give the name of this positive charge
within an atom and describe how scientists' ideas about it have changed over time.

....

....

....

....
[3]

[Total 4 marks]

The Atom

Choose from the words below to fill in the blanks in the passage.

protons   neutrons

compounds
electrons

heavy   light

.... and .... are found in the nucleus of an atom.

.... move around the nucleus in shells.

Compared to electrons, protons and neutrons are ....

1   Atoms are made up of different particles.   Grade 1-3

a) Complete **Figure 1**.

Particle	Relative Charge
Proton	....
....	0
Electron	....

Figure 1

[3]

b) The relative mass of a proton is 1. What is the relative mass of a neutron?

....

[1]

[Total 4 marks]

2   The mass and charge of an atom depends on its subatomic particles.   Grade 4-5

a) Name the region where most of the mass of the atom is concentrated.

....

[1]

b) Use the relative charges of the subatomic particles to
explain why an atom has no overall charge.

....

....

....

....

[3]

[Total 4 marks]

Section 10 — Key Concepts in Chemistry

Atomic Number, Mass Number and Isotopes

1 A potassium atom can be represented by the nuclear symbol $^{39}_{19}K$. **Grade 4-5**

a) State the mass number and atomic number of $^{39}_{19}K$.

mass number: ....

atomic number: ....

[2]

b) How many protons, neutrons and electrons does an atom of $^{39}_{19}K$ have?

protons: ....   neutrons: ....   electrons: ....

[3]

[Total 5 marks]

2 Isotopes are different forms of the same element. **Grade 4-5**

a) Bromine has two stable isotopes, A and B. **Figure 1** shows some information about them. Complete **Figure 1** by calculating the number of neutrons and electrons for each isotope.

isotope	mass number	number of protons	number of neutrons	number of electrons
A	79	35	....	....
B	81	35	....	....

Figure 1

[2]

b) **Figure 2** shows the nuclear symbols for two atoms.

$$^{54}_{26}X \qquad ^{54}_{24}Y$$

Figure 2

Are the atoms in **Figure 2** isotopes? Give a reason for your answer.

....

....

....

[2]

[Total 4 marks]

Exam Practice Tip

Don't let isotopes confuse you. Just because they've got different numbers of neutrons, a pair of isotopes will still have the same number of protons. This means they have the same atomic number but different mass numbers. Simple.

The Periodic Table

1   **Figure 1** shows the periodic table.

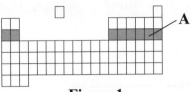

Figure 1

a) How are the elements ordered in the periodic table?

....

[1]

b) What are the vertical columns in the periodic table called?

....

[1]

c) Period 3 is shaded grey. How many electron shells does element A have?

....

[1]

[Total 3 marks]

2*   Dmitri Mendeleev made one of the first periodic tables.

Describe how Mendeleev arranged the elements in his table.
In your answer, you should describe how he used his table to predict the existence
and properties of some elements that hadn't been discovered at the time.

....

....

....

....

....

....

....

....

....

....

[Total 6 marks]

Electronic Configurations

1   Complete **Figure 1** to show how many electrons go in each of the first three electron shells.

Electron shell	Number of electrons it can hold
1st	....
2nd	....
3rd	....

Figure 1

[Total 3 marks]

2   Argon has an atomic number of 18.

a) What is the electron configuration of an argon atom? Tick **one** box.

☐ **A** 2, 16   ☐ **B** 2, 14, 2   ☐ **C** 2, 8, 8   ☐ **D** 8, 8, 2

[1]

b) Which shells do electrons fill first in an atom?

....

[1]

[Total 2 marks]

3   Electronic structures can be represented in different ways.

a) **Figure 2** shows the electronic structures of an
    atom of chlorine (Cl), and an atom of boron (B).
    Give the electronic structures of chlorine and boron in number form.

Chlorine: ....

Boron: ....

Chlorine   Boron

Figure 2

[2]

b) Sulfur has an atomic number of 16.
    Complete the diagram to show the electronic structure of sulfur.

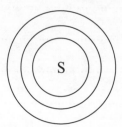

[2]

[Total 4 marks]

Exam Practice Tip

Electronic structures are a key idea in chemistry, so it's important that you understand them. Definitely make sure you know the electronic structures for the first 20 elements in the periodic table. If you can't remember them all, you can work them out by remembering how many electrons can fit in each shell. Doing this will be helpful for your exams.

Ions

1 This question is about ions. (Grade 1-3)

a) Complete the sentence below.
Use a word from the box.

atoms	neutrons	charges

Ions are formed when .... gain or lose electrons.

[1]

b) An ion has a charge of +1.
How many electrons were lost in the formation of this ion?

....

[1]

[Total 2 marks]

2 There are four different ions shown below. Each one is of a different element. (Grade 4-5)

Draw **one** line between each ion and its description.

Ion		**Description**

A^+

D^-

X^{2+}

Z^{2-}

A non-metal from Group 6

A metal from Group 2

A metal from Group 1

A non-metal from Group 0

A non-metal from Group 7

[Total 4 marks]

3 Potassium can react with oxygen to form the ionic compound potassium oxide. (Grade 4-5)

a) What is the overall charge of potassium oxide?

....

[1]

b) Potassium oxide is made up of K^+ and O^{2-} ions.
What is the chemical formula of potassium oxide?

....

[1]

[Total 2 marks]

Ionic Bonding

1   Ionic bonds form when ions are attracted to each other.   *Grade 3-4*

a) Ionic bonds form between positive and negative ions.
   What are the names given to positive and negative ions?

   Positive ions: ....

   Negative ions: ....

   [2]

b) Magnesium and oxygen bond together to form the ionic compound magnesium oxide (MgO).
   To form MgO a magnesium atom **loses** two electrons and an oxygen atom **gains** two electrons.

   State the formulas of the magnesium and oxygen ions in MgO.

   Magnesium ion: ....

   Oxygen ion: ....

   [2]

   [Total 4 marks]

2   **Figure 1** shows the formation of lithium chloride from its elements.   *Grade 4-5*

a) Complete the diagram by:
   • adding an **arrow** to show the transfer of electron(s)
   • adding the charges of the ions
   • completing the outer shell electronic structure of the chloride ion

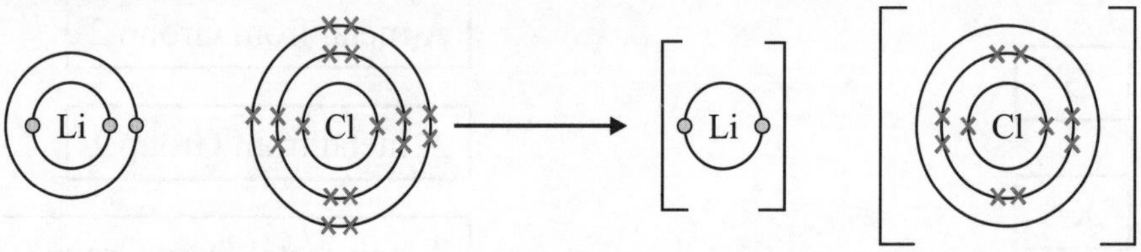

   Figure 1

   [3]

b) Name the force that holds the ions together in an ionic bond.

   ....

   [1]

c) State how you can tell from a dot and cross diagram that the particles in a compound are held
   together by ionic bonds.

   ....

   ....

   [1]

   [Total 5 marks]

Exam Practice Tip

Understanding how ionic compounds are formed can be a bit tricky. Just remember that no electrons disappear, they just move. Make sure you practise drawing some compounds with arrows to show how the electrons move and form the ions.

Ionic Compounds

Warm-Up

Circle the correct words or phrases in the passage below.

In an ionic compound, the particles are held together by <u>weak</u>/<u>strong</u>

forces of attraction. These forces are called ionic bonds and result

in the particles bonding together to form <u>giant lattices</u>/<u>small molecules</u>.

1   Potassium bromide is an ionic compound made of potassium ions and bromide ions.

a) Complete the diagram below to show the position of the ions in potassium bromide.
Write a symbol in each circle to show whether it is a potassium ion (K^+) or a bromide ion (Br^-).

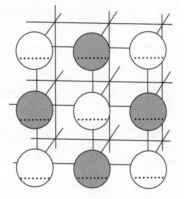

[1]

b) Give **one** disadvantage of using the type of diagram above to show
the structure of an ionic compound.

....

....
[1]
[Total 2 marks]

2   Ionic compounds have similar properties and structures.

a) Name the type of structure that ionic compounds have.

....
[1]

b) State **two** properties of ionic compounds.

1..

2..
[2]
[Total 3 marks]

Covalent Bonding

1   This question is about covalent bonding.

Complete the sentences below. Use words from the box.

outer	share	inner	covalent	electrons	swap

A covalent bond forms when two atoms .... a pair of ....

Atoms form covalent bonds to get a full .... shell of electrons.

[Total 3 marks]

2   There are forces of attraction between molecules in simple molecular substances.

a) Compare the strength of the bonds that hold the atoms in a molecule
together with the forces that exist between different molecules.

....

[1]

b) What happens to the bonds and forces when a simple molecular substance melts?

....

....

[2]

[Total 3 marks]

3   In each molecule of methane (CH_4), one carbon atom is covalently
bonded to four hydrogen atoms. **Figure 1** shows dot and cross
diagrams of the outer shells of hydrogen and carbon atoms.

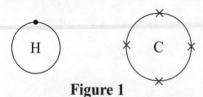

Figure 1

Draw a dot and cross diagram to show the bonding in **one molecule** of methane.
You only need to include the outer shell electrons of each atom.

[Total 2 marks]

Giant Covalent Structures

1   Some molecules have giant covalent structures.   (Grade 3-4)

a) What is meant by the term 'giant covalent structure'?

....
                                                                                                    [1]

b) To melt a giant covalent compound, the covalent bonds between atoms must be broken.
Explain why this causes giant covalent compounds to have very high melting points.

....

....
                                                                                                    [2]

                                                                                      [Total 3 marks]

2   Carbon can form different structures. These include diamond and graphite.   (Grade 4-5)

a) In diamond, how many bonds does each carbon atom form?

....
                                                                                                    [1]

b) Draw **one** line between each of the properties of diamond and its explanation.

Property   **Explanation**

Does not conduct electricity

High melting point

Hard (doesn't scratch easily)

Electrons in covalent bonds cannot move.

Each carbon atom makes multiple strong covalent bonds.

                                                                                                    [2]

c) In graphite, carbon atoms are bonded together in hexagons.
Describe how the hexagons are arranged.

....
                                                                                                    [1]

d) Graphite is often used to make electrodes.
Explain why the structure of graphite makes it suitable for this.

....

....
                                                                                                    [2]

                                                                                      [Total 6 marks]

Polymers and Fullerenes

1   Polymers are commonly used as plastics.   (Grade 1-3)

Complete the sentences below. Use words from the box.

long	small	heavy	dense

In a polymer lots of .... units are joined together

to form a .... molecule.

[Total 2 marks]

2   Three different carbon structures are shown in **Figure 1**.   (Grade 3-4)

Look at the structures labelled **A** and **B**.

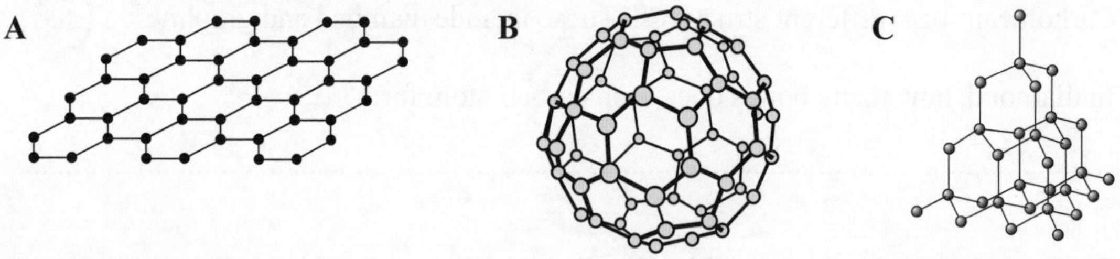

A

B

C

Figure 1

a)   Which of the diagrams above represents each of the following carbon structures?
Write a letter in each box.

Buckminsterfullerene (C_{60}) ☐   Graphene ☐

[2]

b)   Explain why structure **A** can conduct electricity.

....

[1]

[Total 3 marks]

3   **Figure 2** represents a polymer.   (Grade 4-5)

a)   What is the common name of this polymer?

....

[1]

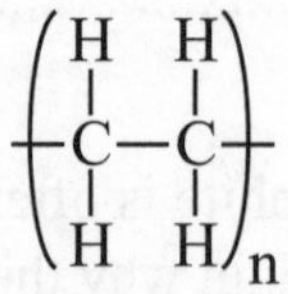

$$\left(\begin{array}{cc} H & H \\ | & | \\ -C & -C- \\ | & | \\ H & H \end{array} \right)_n$$

Figure 2

b)   State what type of bonds hold the atoms in the polymer together.

....

[1]

[Total 2 marks]

Section 10 — Key Concepts in Chemistry

Metallic Bonding

1 State two differences between the properties of metals and non-metals. (Grade 3-4)

1. ....

2. ....

[Total 2 marks]

2 **Figure 1** shows the structure of a metal. (Grade 4-5)

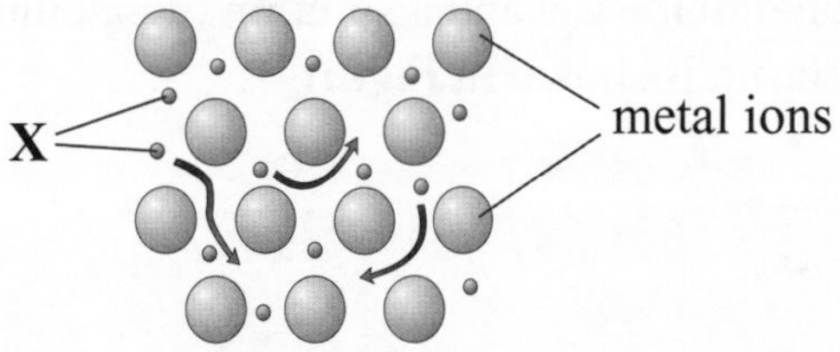

Figure 1

a) In **Figure 1** some particles are labelled with an **X**. Name these particles.

   ....
   [1]

b) Metal atoms form ions that are positively charged.
   Explain how they are held together in the structure seen in **Figure 1**.

   ....

   ....
   [2]

c) Metals have high melting and boiling points. Explain why.

   ....

   ....
   [2]

d) In a pure metal, the atoms are arranged in layers.
   Explain why this means that metals can be bent and shaped.

   ....

   ....
   [1]

   [Total 6 marks]

Exam Practice Tip

Metals have some really nifty properties. You should try to be really familiar with metallic bonding, so that you can explain all the properties of metals. Remember, it's because of those layers of positive metal ions and those free electrons that metals behave the way they do. Make sure you're able to explain the bonding in metals and link it to their properties.

Section 10 — Key Concepts in Chemistry

Conservation of Mass

1   A student mixes 3.0 g of silver nitrate solution and 15.0 g of sodium chloride solution together in a flask and seals it with a bung. The following precipitation reaction occurs:

$$AgNO_{3\,(aq)} + NaCl_{(aq)} \rightarrow AgCl_{(s)} + NaNO_{3\,(aq)}$$

Predict the total mass of the contents of the flask after the reaction.

....

[Total 1 mark]

2   A student is investigating a reaction between calcium carbonate and hydrochloric acid. The reaction produces carbon dioxide gas and a solution of calcium chloride. The student's experimental set-up is shown in **Figure 1**.

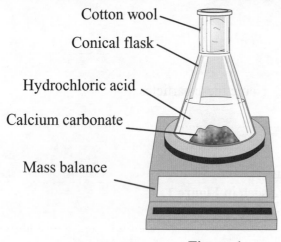

Cotton wool

Conical flask

Hydrochloric acid

Calcium carbonate

Mass balance

Figure 1

mass at the start of the reaction:

mass at the end of the reaction:

Figure 2

a) Calculate the change in mass of the reaction container during the reaction.

Change in mass = ... g

[1]

b) The student thinks that the measurements must be wrong, because no mass is lost or gained in a chemical reaction. Is the student correct? Explain your answer.

....

....

....

....

....

[4]

[Total 5 marks]

Relative Masses

1 The relative atomic mass of chlorine is 35.5. The relative atomic mass of hydrogen is 1. Grade 3-4

a) Calculate the relative formula mass of hydrochloric acid (HCl).

Relative formula mass = ...
[1]

b) Calculate the relative formula mass of chlorine gas (Cl_2).

Relative formula mass = ...
[1]

[Total 2 marks]

2 Match up the following formulas with the correct relative formula mass of the substance. Grade 4-5

F_2

C_2H_6

NaOH

38

36

40

30

56

[Total 3 marks]

3 When magnesium is heated in air, magnesium oxide is produced. Grade 4-5
The balanced equation for this reaction is: $2Mg + O_2 \rightarrow 2MgO$

a) Calculate the relative formula mass (M_r) of magnesium oxide.
(relative atomic masses: O = 16, Mg = 24)

Relative formula mass = ...
[1]

b) Calculate the mass of magnesium oxide produced when 48 g of magnesium is heated.

Mass of magnesium oxide = ... g
[3]

[Total 4 marks]

Section 10 — Key Concepts in Chemistry

78

Calculating Empirical Formulas

Warm-Up

Complete the sentences below using words from the box.

| largest | atoms | molecular | empirical |

The .... formula tells you the smallest whole number ratio

of .... in a compound. You can work it out using the

.... formula for a compound.

1 A hydrocarbon has the molecular formula C_2H_4.
What is the empirical formula for this compound? Tick **one** box.

Grade
1-3

☐ **A** CH_2 ☐ **B** C_4H_8 ☐ **C** C_2H ☐ **D** CH

[Total 1 mark]

2 A compound has the empirical formula C_2H_6N. Which of the following
could be the molecular formula of the compound? Tick **one** box.

Grade
3-4

☐ **A** CH_3N ☐ **B** $C_4H_6N_2$ ☐ **C** $C_6H_2N_3$ ☐ **D** $C_4H_{12}N_2$

[Total 1 mark]

3 Decaborane is a compound with the molecular formula $B_{10}H_{14}$.

Grade
3-4

What is the empirical formula of decaborane?

empirical formula = ...

[Total 1 mark]

4 Compound Q has the empirical formula CH_2.
The relative formula mass of compound Q is 42.

Grade
4-5

What is the molecular formula of compound Q?
(relative atomic masses: H = 1, C = 12)

molecular formula = ...

[Total 3 marks]

5   Compound X contains 2 g of hydrogen and 32 g of oxygen.

a) Calculate the empirical formula of compound X.
(relative atomic masses: H = 1, O = 16)

empirical formula = ...
[3]

b) The M_r of compound X is 34. By finding the M_r of the empirical formula,
calculate the molecular formula of compound X.

molecular formula = ...
[3]

[Total 6 marks]

6   A student heated some magnesium, as shown in **Figure 1**. When heated,
magnesium reacts with oxygen to produce magnesium oxide.

The student measured the mass of the reaction container before adding the magnesium and at the
start and end of the reaction. The results of the experiment are shown in **Figure 2**.

	Mass (g)
mass of magnesium	1.32
mass of magnesium oxide	2.20

Figure 2

Figure 1

a) Calculate the mass of oxygen in the magnesium oxide produced during the experiment.

mass = ... g
[1]

b) Calculate the empirical formula of magnesium oxide.

empirical formula = ...
[3]

[Total 4 marks]

Exam Practice Tip

When you get given some masses and asked to work out an empirical formula, the first step is always to divide the
mass of each element by its relative atomic mass. Then, you can work out the smallest whole number ratio between the
relative amounts of each element. And... hey presto, you can use that ratio to write the empirical formula.

Concentration

Some units are listed in the table on the right.

Put a tick in the correct column to show whether each unit is a unit of mass or a unit of volume.

Unit	Mass	Volume
g		
cm^3		
dm^3		
kg		

1 Solution X is made by dissolving 1 g of solid in 1 dm^3 of water. *(Grade 3-4)*

Which of these solutions will be **more** concentrated than solution X?
Tick **one** box.

☐ **A** 1 g of solid in 2 dm^3 of water   ☐ **C** 1 g of solid in 3 dm^3 of water

☐ **B** 0.5 g of solid in 1 dm^3 of water   ☐ **D** 2 g of solid in 1 dm^3 of water

[Total 1 mark]

2 28 g of calcium chloride was dissolved in 400 cm^3 of water. *(Grade 4-5)*

a) Calculate the concentration of the solution in g dm^{-3}.

Concentration = ... g dm^{-3}
[2]

b) Explain the term 'concentration of a solution'.

....

....
[1]

c) A student needs another solution of calcium chloride, this time with a concentration of 50 g dm^{-3}.
What mass of calcium chloride do they need to add to 0.2 dm^3 of water to make this solution?
Use the equation: mass = concentration × volume

Mass = ... g
[2]

[Total 5 marks]

Exam Practice Tip

For questions about concentrations, you'll probably need the formula that links concentration, mass and volume. It's a good idea to write down this formula triangle before you start. Then cover up the thing you want to find, to work out how to calculate it from the values you do know.

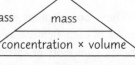

Section 10 — Key Concepts in Chemistry

States of Matter

Warm-Up

Identify which of the following statements is **false**. Tick **one** box.

- Particles in solids can't move around but they vibrate. ☐
- There is hardly any force of attraction between particles in gases. ☐
- Particles in liquids are held in fixed positions by strong forces. ☐

1 Most substances exist in one of three states of matter. These are solids, liquids and gases. **Figure 1** shows how particles are arranged in each of the three states. (Grade 1-3)

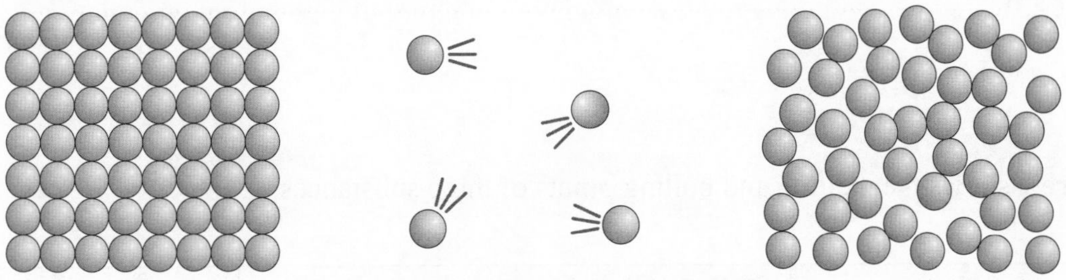

A B C

Figure 1

a) Which of the states shown in **Figure 1** represents a liquid? Give your answer as **A**, **B** or **C**.

....

[1]

b) In **Figure 1**, what does each ball represent?

....

[1]

[Total 2 marks]

2 The particles in each state of matter have different amounts of energy. (Grade 4-5)

a) Place solids, liquids and gases in order of the amount of energy that their particles have.

Most energy ....

↕ ....

Least energy ....

[1]

b) When gases and liquids are placed inside a container they change shape.
Explain why this does **not** happen when a solid is put inside a container.

....

....

[1]

[Total 2 marks]

Changes of State

1   Substances can change from one state to another.

In **Figure 1** the arrows represent processes that cause a change in state to happen.

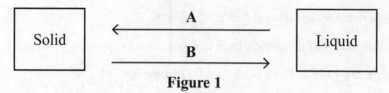

Figure 1

Name the processes **A** and **B**.

Process **A**: ....

Process **B**: ....

[Total 2 marks]

2   **Figure 2** shows the melting and boiling points of three substances.

Substance	Sodium Chloride	Water	Copper
Melting Point (°C)	801	0	1083
Boiling Point (°C)	1413	100	2567

Figure 2

a) Which substance in **Figure 2** would be a liquid at 900 °C?

....

[1]

b) Which two substances in **Figure 2** would be gases at 1500 °C?

1. ....

2. ....

[2]

c) When a substance evaporates into a gas it undergoes a physical change.
Describe the difference between a physical and a chemical change.

....

....

[2]

[Total 5 marks]

Exam Practice Tip

You need to be able to predict what state a substance will be in certain conditions. Just remember, if the given
temperature is lower than the melting point of the substance, the substance will be a solid. If it's higher than the melting
point, the substance will be a liquid and if it's higher than the boiling point, the substance will be a gas.

Section 11 — States of Matter and Mixtures

Purity

1 Chemists sometimes need samples of pure substances. (Grade 3-4)

a) How is a pure substance defined in chemistry? Tick **one** box.

☐ **A** A single element not mixed with any other substance.

☐ **B** A single compound not mixed with any other substance.

☐ **C** A single element or compound not mixed with any other substance.

☐ **D** An element that has not been reacted with anything.

[1]

b) **Figure 1** shows some different substances.
Which of these substances are pure and which are mixtures?
Tick **one** box in each row.

Substance	Pure	Mixture
Sea water		
Deionised water		
Copper		
Copper oxide		

Figure 1

[4]

[Total 5 marks]

2 A scientist is comparing samples of two substances.
One sample is a pure compound, but the other is a mixture.
Both substances are solids at room temperature. (Grade 4-5)

a) The scientist decides to work out which is the pure compound by heating both
samples and recording their melting points. Explain how she will be able to tell
which is the pure compound, even if she does not know its melting point.

....

....

....

[2]

b) Suggest what apparatus the scientist could use to
measure the melting points of the substances in the lab.

....

[1]

[Total 3 marks]

Distillation

1 **Figure 1** shows a set of equipment that could be used to desalinate sea water.

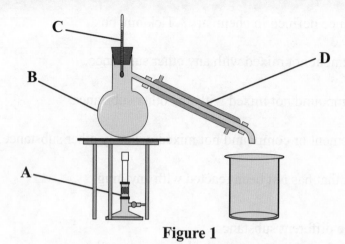

Figure 1

a) Name the components labelled **A** to **D** in **Figure 1**. Use the words in the box.

round bottomed flask	condenser	evaporating dish
Bunsen burner	**filter funnel**	**thermometer**

A .... B ....

C .... D ....

[4]

b) What separation technique could the apparatus be used for? Tick **one** box.

☐ **A** Evaporation ☐ **B** Condensation ☐ **C** Simple distillation ☐ **D** Fractional distillation

[1]

[Total 5 marks]

2 A student is using fractional distillation to separate a mixture of liquids. She puts the mixture in a flask and attaches a fractionating column and condenser above the flask.

Figure 2 shows the next steps in the experiment.
Write numbers in the boxes to show the order the steps are carried out in.
The first one has been done for you.

Step	Order
The flask is heated slowly.	1
The first liquid is collected.	
The heat of the flask is increased.	
The substance with lowest boiling point evaporates and rises up the column.	
The substance with lowest boiling point condenses and runs down the condenser.	

Figure 2

[Total 4 marks]

Filtration and Crystallisation

1 Filtration is a way of separating substances.

a) Complete the sentence below that describes filtration.
   Use words from the box.

soluble	insoluble	solids	liquids	gases

Filtration is used to separate .... solids from ....

[2]

b) Which piece of equipment would you use in a filtration experiment? Tick **one** box.

☐ **A** Evaporating dish   ☐ **B** Bunsen burner   ☐ **C** Funnel   ☐ **D** Condenser

[1]

[Total 3 marks]

2 A student wants to separate the components of a mixture.
The mixture is a white powder composed of barium sulfate and potassium iodide.
Figure 1 shows some information about the two compounds in the mixture.

Name	Appearance at room temperature	Soluble in water?
barium sulfate	white solid	no
potassium iodide	white solid	yes

Figure 1

The student mixes the powder with water and then carries out a filtration.

a) Which solid compound will he separate out using this method?

....

[1]

b)* The student separates the remaining compound by crystallisation and filtration.
   Describe a method for this technique.

....

....

....

....

....

....

....

[6]

[Total 7 marks]

Section 11 — States of Matter and Mixtures

86

Chromatography

PRACTICAL

Warm-Up

Use the words to label the different parts of the chromatography experiment shown on the right.

baseline
filter paper
spots of chemicals
solvent front

....

....

....

....

1 A scientist analysed three dyes, **D**, **E** and **F** using paper chromatography. Ethanol was used as the solvent.

Grade 4-5

a) During the experiment the scientist placed a watch glass on top of the beaker. Give **one** reason why he might have done this.

....

[1]

b) The experiment had two phases. What was the mobile phase in this experiment?

☐ **A** The filter paper

☐ **B** The dyes

☐ **C** The baseline

☐ **D** The ethanol

[1]

c) The chromatogram produced in the experiment is shown in **Figure 1**.

D E F

Figure 1

Explain why the dyes have formed spots at different places on the filter paper.

....

....

[1]

[Total 3 marks]

Section 11 — States of Matter and Mixtures

Interpreting Chromatograms

1   A scientist used chromatography and simple distillation to analyse an ink
    called sunrise yellow. He ran pure samples of four reference substances
    (**A – D**) next to the ink. The results are shown in **Figure 1**.
    The boiling points of some solvents are shown in **Figure 2**.

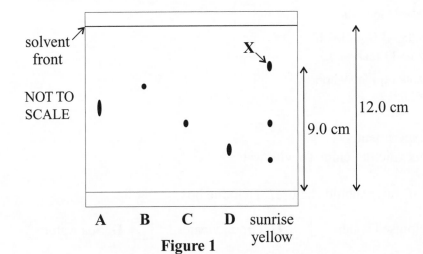

Solvent	Boiling point (°C)
ethanol	78
water	100
ethyl acetate	77
methanol	65

Figure 2

a) The scientist finds that the boiling point of the solvent in sunrise yellow is 100 °C.
    Use **Figure 2** to predict what the solvent is.

    ....
    [1]

b) The reference substances are pure samples.
    Explain how you can tell this from the chromatogram in **Figure 1**.

    ....
    [1]

c) Which of the reference substances, **A-D**, could be present in sunrise yellow?

    ....
    [1]

d) Describe how you could check whether sunrise yellow contains
    the reference substance you identified in part c).

    ....

    ....

    ....
    [2]

e) Calculate the R_f value for the spot of chemical labelled **X** in **Figure 1**.
    Use the equation: $R_f = \dfrac{\text{distance moved by substance}}{\text{distance moved by solvent}}$

    R_f = ...
    [2]

    [Total 7 marks]

Water Treatment

Tick the boxes to show whether the following statements are **true** or **false**.

	True	False
Potable water is the same as drinking water.	☐	☐
Potable water can only be produced from fresh water found in rivers, streams and reservoirs.	☐	☐
Sea water can be made drinkable by distillation.	☐	☐

1   A student is doing a chemistry experiment.
The method says she needs to mix calcium chloride with water. **Grade 3-4**

a) Which of the following sources of water should she use? Tick **one** box.

☐ **A** Tap water   ☐ **B** Deionised water   ☐ **C** Ground water   ☐ **D** Sea water

[1]

b) Explain why it is important to use pure water in experiments.

....

....

[2]

[Total 3 marks]

2   A purification plant uses multiple steps to purify water. **Figure 1** shows
the three stages water goes through at a water purification plant. **Grade 4-5**

$$\boxed{\text{X}} \longrightarrow \boxed{\text{Sedimentation}} \longrightarrow \boxed{\text{Chlorination}}$$

Figure 1

a) During stage **X**, the water is passed through wire meshes and gravel beds
to remove large solid impurities. Give the name of this step.

....

[1]

b) What happens during the stage described as 'sedimentation'?

....

....

[2]

c) Explain why chlorine gas is bubbled through the water during chlorination.

....

[1]

[Total 4 marks]

Acids and Bases

Fill in the gaps in the following statements.

acids

bases

neutral

Substances with a pH of less than 7 are ....

Substances with a pH of 7 are ....

1   **Figure 1** shows the pH of some everyday substances.   **Grade 3-4**

Substance	Beer	Bicarbonate of Soda	Water
pH	4	9	7

Figure 1

a) Write the name of the substance in **Figure 1** that is an acid.

    ....

    [1]

b) What colour would you expect phenolphthalein to turn in bicarbonate of soda solution?

    ....

    [1]

    [Total 2 marks]

2   The pH of a substance tells you whether it's an acid or a base.   **Grade 4-5**

a) Which ion is always produced by an acid in aqueous solution? Tick **one** box.

    ☐ **A** Cl^-

    ☐ **B** H^+

    ☐ **C** OH^-

    ☐ **D** OH^+

    [1]

b) What is a base?

    ....

    [1]

c) Some bases are soluble in water. State the term for these types of bases.

    ....

    [1]

d) State the range of the pH scale.

    ....

    [2]

    [Total 5 marks]

Neutralisation Reactions

1   A student monitors how the pH of a reaction mixture changes when calcium oxide is added to hydrochloric acid.   Grade 3-4   PRACTICAL

a)   State what could be used to monitor the pH of the solution during the reaction.

....
[1]

b)   **Figure 1** shows the student's results. Plot a graph to show how the pH changed in the experiment.

Mass of base added (g)	pH
0	1.0
0.2	1.0
0.4	1.5
0.6	2.0
0.8	3.5
1.0	5.5
1.2	6.5
1.4	7.0
1.6	7.0
1.8	7.0

Figure 1

pH

mass of calcium hydroxide added (g)

[2]

c)   Use your graph to describe how the pH changes as the base is added to the acid.

....

....

....

....
[4]

[Total 7 marks]

2   Acids and bases react together in neutralisation reactions.   Grade 4-5

a)   Write the word equation for a neutralisation reaction between an acid and a base.

.... + ... → .... + ...
[1]

b)   Write an equation that shows how hydrogen (H^+) and hydroxide (OH^-) ions react together in a neutralisation reaction.

.... + ... → ....
[1]

c)   State the pH of the products that form when an acid reacts with an alkali.

....
[1]

[Total 3 marks]

Reactions of Acids

1   Draw **one** line from each acid to the type of salt it forms when it reacts with a base.   Grade 1-3

Acid	Salt

Hydrochloric acid   Nitrate

Nitric acid   Sulfate

Sulfuric acid   Chloride

[Total 2 marks]

2   Acids react with metal carbonates to form a salt and two other products.   Grade 3-4

a)   Other than a salt, name the **two** products that are formed
when an acid reacts with a metal carbonate.

1. ....

2. ....

[2]

b)   A student reacts zinc carbonate with dilute hydrochloric acid.
What is the name of the salt produced in this reaction? Tick **one** box.

☐   **A**   zinc hydroxide

☐   **B**   zinc sulfate

☐   **C**   zinc chloride

☐   **D**   zinc nitrate

[1]

[Total 3 marks]

3   A student performs an experiment that produces a colourless gas.
To identify the gas, she collects it and carries out tests.   Grade 4-5

a)   Describe a test the student could carry out to investigate whether the gas is carbon dioxide.
Include the observation the student would make if carbon dioxide was present.

Test: ....

Observation: ....

[2]

b)   When the student holds a lighted splint in the gas, she hears a squeaky pop. Name the gas.

....

[1]

[Total 3 marks]

☹ ☐   ☺ ☐   ☺ ☐

Making Soluble Salts

Circle the substances below that are salts.

sulfuric acid   sodium chloride   hydrochloric acid   water

copper nitrate   carbon dioxide   zinc sulfate

1   A student is making the salt potassium chloride. **Figure 1** shows the set-up of his experiment.

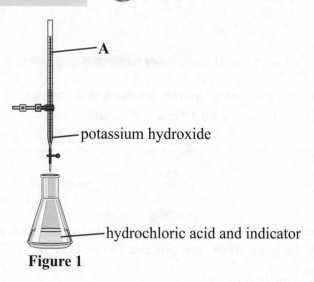

Figure 1

a) Name the piece of equipment labelled **A**.

....

[1]

b) The student adds potassium hydroxide to the hydrochloric acid until all the acid has reacted. How can the student tell that all the acid has reacted?

....

[1]

To get a solution containing only potassium chloride, the student repeats the experiment. He uses the same volumes of hydrochloric acid and potassium hydroxide. This time he doesn't add indicator to the acid.

c) Explain why the student must be careful to use the same amounts of hydrochloric acid and potassium hydroxide.

....

[1]

d) Explain why the student doesn't add indicator to the second reaction.

....

[1]

[Total 4 marks]

2 Salts can be soluble or insoluble in water. (Grade 3-4)

a) What does it mean if a salt is soluble in water?

....

[1]

b) Complete the sentences below. Use words from the box.

| soluble | insoluble | sulfate | lead | iron | hydroxide |

All nitrate salts are .... in water.

Most chloride salts are soluble in water, except for silver chloride and .... chloride.

Most .... salts are insoluble in water.

[3]

c) A student puts some zinc sulfate in water. What would you expect to happen?

....

[1]

[Total 5 marks]

3 A student makes the soluble salt copper sulfate by reacting insoluble copper oxide with sulfuric acid. (Grade 4-5) **PRACTICAL**

Write a method for producing pure crystals of the salt using this reaction.

• Describe how you would make the salt from the reactants.
• Describe how you would purify the salt from the reaction mixture.

....

....

....

....

....

....

....

....

[Total 4 marks]

Exam Practice Tip

Knowing which salts are soluble and which are insoluble is really important for working out the best way to make them. So make sure you've brushed up on the solubility rules before you go into the exams.

Section 12 — Chemical Changes

Making Insoluble Salts

1 Insoluble salts can be made by precipitation reactions.
Which of the following equations shows a precipitation reaction? Tick **one** box.

Grade 3-4

☐ **A** $CuO_{(s)} + 2HCl_{(aq)} \rightarrow CuCl_{2\,(aq)} + H_2O_{(l)}$

☐ **B** $HCl_{(aq)} + NaOH_{(aq)} \rightarrow NaCl_{(aq)} + H_2O_{(l)}$

☐ **C** $2HNO_{3\,(aq)} + ZnCO_{3\,(s)} \rightarrow Zn(NO_3)_{2\,(aq)} + H_2O_{(l)} + CO_{2\,(g)}$

☐ **D** $Pb(NO_3)_{2\,(aq)} + 2NaCl_{(aq)} \rightarrow PbCl_{2\,(s)} + 2NaNO_{3\,(aq)}$

[Total 1 mark]

2 A student reacts iron nitrate solution with sodium hydroxide solution to make an insoluble salt containing iron.

Grade 4-5

a) Name the insoluble salt that forms.

....

[1]

b) Describe how the student could prepare the iron nitrate solution from solid iron nitrate.

....

....

[2]

c) The student used the following method to prepare the salt:

1. Mix the sodium hydroxide solution with the iron(III) nitrate solution in a beaker and stir.
2. Line a filter funnel with filter paper and place it in a conical flask.
   Pour the contents of the beaker into the filter paper.
3. Rinse the beaker with deionised water and tip this into the filter paper.
4. Rinse the contents of the filter paper with deionised water.

i) Describe what the student would see during step 1.

....

[1]

ii) What is the purpose of step 3?

....

[1]

iii) Explain why the student used deionised water to rinse the salt.

....

[1]

[Total 6 marks]

Electrolysis

1 A student sets up an electrochemical cell as shown in **Figure 1**.

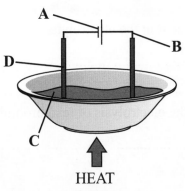

HEAT
Figure 1

a) Use words from the box to name the pieces of equipment labelled A-D.

| power supply   electrode   wire   electron   molten ionic compound   crucible |

A: ....   B: ....

C: ....   D: ....

[4]

b) The student carries out the electrolysis in a fume cupboard.
Suggest an explanation for why she does this.

....

[1]

[Total 5 marks]

2 Electrochemical cells contain electrodes in an electrolyte.
The electrolyte can be a liquid or a solution.

a) What are the electrodes? Tick **one** box.

☐ **A** Solids that conduct electricity.

☐ **B** Solids that react with the electrolyte.

☐ **C** Solids that don't conduct electricity.

☐ **D** Solid ionic compounds.

[1]

b) Complete the passage below about electrodes. Use words from the box.
You can use words more than once.

| positive   anode   cathode   negative   neutral |

In electrolysis, the anode is the .... electrode. .... ions move to the

anode. The cathode is the .... electrode. .... ions move to the cathode.

[4]

[Total 5 marks]

3 Lead bromide can be electrolysed. The electrolyte is molten lead bromide. (Grade 4-5)

a) What is an electrolyte?

....

[2]

b) State the ions that will be present in the electrolyte.

....

[1]

c) Write the word equation for the electrolysis of lead bromide.

.... → .... + ...

[1]

[Total 4 marks]

4 Copper sulfate can be electrolysed using inert electrodes or using copper electrodes. (Grade 4-5)

a) Draw **one** line from each type of electrode to the products that are formed when they are used.

PRACTICAL

Electrodes	Products of electrolysis

inert electrodes

copper electrodes

Copper and sulfur

Oxygen gas and copper metal

Copper and copper ions

[2]

b) A student electrolysed copper sulfate solution using copper electrodes. She recorded the masses of the dry electrodes before and after the electrolysis. Her results are shown in **Figure 2**.

Electrode	Initial Mass (g)	Final Mass (g)
Anode	8.21	7.19
Cathode	7.56	8.48

Figure 2

i) Explain why the student weighed the electrodes when they were dry.

....

[1]

ii) Calculate the change in mass of the cathode.

Change in mass = ... g

[1]

c) During electrolysis, there is a flow of charge through the electrolyte. What causes this flow of charge?

....

[1]

[Total 5 marks]

Section 12 — Chemical Changes

5   Aqueous sodium chloride solution can be electrolysed using inert electrodes.   (Grade 4-5)

a) What ions are present in sodium chloride solution? Tick **one** box.

☐ **A** Na^+, Cl^-

☐ **B** OH^+, O^{2-}, Na^+, Cl^-

☐ **C** H^+, OH^-, Na^+, Cl^-

☐ **D** H^+, O^{2-}, Na^+, Cl^-

[1]

b) Explain why hydrogen, not sodium, is formed at the cathode.

....

[1]

c) State what element is formed at the anode.

....

[1]

d) Molten sodium chloride can also be electrolysed.
Predict the products when molten sodium chloride is electrolysed using inert electrodes.

....

[2]

[Total 5 marks]

6*   Explain how copper can be purified using electrolysis.   (Grade 4-5)

In your answer, you should describe:
• What the electrodes are made from.
• How the copper moves during the reaction.
• What happens to the impurities.

....

....

....

....

....

....

....

....

[Total 6 marks]

Exam Practice Tip

Remember, when you electrolyse a salt solution, different substances will be formed at the electrodes depending on how reactive they are. If the metal's <u>more</u> reactive than hydrogen, hydrogen will form. If the metal's <u>less</u> reactive than hydrogen, the metal will form. At the anode, oxygen will form unless there are halide ions in the solution.

 ☐   ☐   ☐

The Reactivity Series

1 **Figure 1** shows part of the reactivity series of metals. Grade 3-4

Potassium	K
Sodium	Na
Magnesium	Mg
Copper	Cu

Figure 1

a) Name **one** metal from **Figure 1** that is less reactive than magnesium.

....

[1]

b) Which metal in **Figure 1** forms positive ions most easily?

....

[1]

[Total 2 marks]

2 Iron can be extracted from its ore by reduction with carbon. The equation for this reaction is shown below. Grade 4-5

$$2Fe_2O_3 + 3C \rightarrow 4Fe + 3CO_2$$

a) What is reduction?

....

[1]

b) Which element is oxidised in this reaction? Give a reason for your answer.

Element: ....

Reason: ....

[2]

[Total 3 marks]

3 When a metal is burnt in oxygen, a metal oxide is formed. This can be described as an oxidation reaction. Explain why, using ideas about the transfer of oxygen. Grade 4-5

....

....

....

[Total 2 marks]

Reactivity of Metals

1   A student had two metals, A and B. He added the same amount of each metal to separate beakers containing the same amount of water. When metal A was added, the temperature of the water increased by 1.5 °C. When metal B was added, the temperature of the water increased by 1.2 °C.

a) Which metal is more reactive?

....

[1]

b) Give **one** way that the student could use an acid to investigate the reactivity of metals A and B that does **not** involve measuring a change in temperature.

....

[1]

[Total 2 marks]

2   A student reacts different metals with water.
The results of this experiment are shown in **Figure 1**.

Reaction	Observation
Copper + water	No reaction
Calcium + water	Fizzing, calcium disappears
Lithium + water	Very vigorous reaction with fizzing, lithium disappears
Magnesium + water	No fizzing, a few bubbles on the magnesium

Figure 1

a) Write the word equation for the reaction of calcium and water.

.... + ... → .... + ...

[1]

b) Use **Figure 1** to put the metals copper, calcium, lithium and magnesium in order of reactivity.

Most reactive .... Least reactive

[2]

c) State **one** thing the student should do to make sure the experiment is fair.

....

[1]

d) The student then adds a piece of magnesium to a solution of copper chloride.
A displacement reaction takes place. Predict the products of this reaction.

....

[2]

e) State how you can predict whether a displacement reaction will take place between a metal and a metal compound.

....

[1]

[Total 7 marks]

Section 13 — Extracting Metals and Equilibria

Extracting Metals Using Carbon

1   Aluminium and gold are two metals found in the Earth's crust. **(Grade 1-3)**

   a) What is the term given to the process of separating a metal from its ore?

   ....

                                                                                                 [1]

   b) Complete the sentences using the words below.

common	ore	uncombined element
reactive	rare	unreactive

   Aluminium is .... , so is found in Earth's crust as an ....

   Gold is .... , so is found in Earth's crust as an ....

                                                                                          [4]

                                                                                                   [Total 5 marks]

2   Part of the reactivity series of metals is shown in **Figure 1**. **(Grade 3-4)** Carbon has also been included.

Potassium K
Calcium Ca
Carbon C
Zinc Zn

Figure 1

   a) Name **one** metal from **Figure 1** which could be extracted from its ore by reduction with carbon.

   ....

                                                                                          [1]

   b) Name **one** metal from **Figure 1** which could **not** be extracted from its ore by reduction with carbon. Give a reason for your answer.

   Metal: ....

   Reason: ....

                                                                                               [2]

                                                                                  [Total 3 marks]

3   Iron and sodium are extracted using different methods. **(Grade 4-5)** Describe the difference between how sodium and iron are extracted from their ores. Give a reason for your answer.

   ....

   ....

   ....

                                                                                                     [Total 3 marks]

Extracting Metals Using Electrolysis

1 Magnesium is a metal that can be extracted from its ore using electrolysis. **Grade 4-5**

a) Why is electrolysis used to extract magnesium from its ore?

....
[1]

b) Pure magnesium is more expensive to buy than many metals.
Give **two** reasons why extracting magnesium using electrolysis is expensive.

1. ....

2. ....
[2]

[Total 3 marks]

2 **Figure 1** shows the extraction of aluminium. Aluminium oxide is mixed with cryolite. This mixture is then melted and electrolysed to form metallic aluminium and oxygen gas. **Grade 4-5**

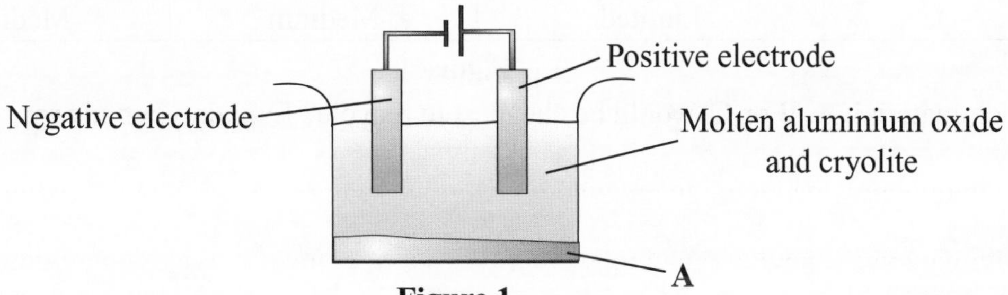

Negative electrode — Positive electrode

Molten aluminium oxide and cryolite

A

Figure 1

a) What is the liquid labelled **A**?

....
[1]

b) Mixing with cryolite lowers the melting point of the aluminium ore.
What effect would this have on the cost of extracting aluminium?

....
[1]

c) Write a **balanced** equation for the conversion of aluminium oxide (Al_2O_3)
to aluminium metal and oxygen using electrolysis.

....
[2]

[Total 4 marks]

Exam Practice Tip

The method that's used to extract a metal from its ore depends on where the metal is in the reactivity series. If the metal's below carbon, it can be extracted by reduction with carbon. If it's above carbon, it's extracted using electrolysis.

Recycling

1 Some materials can be recycled into new products.
Which of the following statements about recycling is false? Tick **one** box.

Grade 3-4

☐ **A** Recycling materials reduces the amount of waste sent to landfill.

☐ **B** Recycling often costs more money than making new materials.

☐ **C** Recycling materials often uses less energy than making new materials.

☐ **D** Recycling materials saves some of the finite amount of resources in the Earth.

[Total 1 mark]

2 Radia is sorting some rubbish around her house.

Grade 4-5

Radia has three pieces of rubbish made from three different materials, **A**, **B** and **C**.
Some data about the materials is in **Figure 1**.

Material	Availability of resource	Energy to recycle	Energy to extract
A	Abundant	High	Low
B	Limited	Low	High
C	Limited	Medium	Medium

Figure 1

a) Which material, **A**, **B** or **C**, would be cheapest to recycle? Explain your answer.

....

....

[2]

b) Give **three** reasons why it may not be worthwhile recycling material **A**.

1. ....

2. ....

3. ....

[3]

c) The energy used to extract materials comes from burning fossil fuels.
Suggest **one** reason why high energy extraction processes may be a problem.

....

....

[1]

d) Which material, **B** or **C**, would you recommend for recycling? Give a reason for your answer.

Material: ....

Reason: ....

[1]

[Total 7 marks]

☹ ☐   🙂 ☐   😊 ☐

Life Cycle Assessments

1   What is the purpose of a life cycle assessment? Tick **one** box.   (Grade 1-3)

   ☐   **A**   It looks at how many different chemicals are used during the life cycle of a product.

   ☐   **B**   It looks at the total amount of greenhouse gases produced during the life cycle of a product.

   ☐   **C**   It looks at every stage of a product's life to assess the impact on the environment.

   ☐   **D**   It looks at the total economic impact of each stage of a product's life.

[Total 1 mark]

2   A mobile phone company is carrying out a life cycle assessment for one of their products.   (Grade 3-4)

a)   Describe **one** environmental problem that may be related to using metals as a raw material.

....

[1]

b)   Suggest **one** environmental impact of disposing of the phone when it no longer works.

....

....

[1]

[Total 2 marks]

3   A new shop is deciding whether to stock plastic bags or paper bags.
To help them decide, they carry out a life cycle assessment for each type of bag.   (Grade 4-5)
Some information about each bag is shown in **Figure 1**.

	Plastic bag	**Paper bag**
Raw materials	Crude oil	Wood
Manufacture	A little waste produced.	Lots of waste produced.
Using the product	Can be reused several times.	Usually only used once.
Disposal	Recyclable Not biodegradable	Recyclable Biodegradable

Figure 1

a)   Using the information in **Figure 1**, give **two** advantages of plastic bags over paper bags.

1. ....

2. ....

[2]

b)   Give **two** other pieces of information, that are not given in **Figure 1**, that would
be needed to help decide which bag has the least impact on the environment.

1. ....

2. ....

[2]

[Total 4 marks]

☹ ☐   ☺ ☐   ☺ ☐   **Section 13 — Extracting Metals and Equilibria**

Dynamic Equilibrium

Circle the correct conditions used in the Haber process.

Temperature: 200 °C / 450 °C   Pressure: 250 atm / 200 atm   Catalyst: iron / aluminium

1 The Haber process is used to make ammonia.

a) Use the correct symbol in the equation to show that the Haber process is a reversible reaction.

$$N_2 + 3 H_2 \ \text{................} \ 2 NH_3$$

[1]

b) Draw **one** line from each reactant in the Haber process to show where it's normally obtained from.

Reactant   **Source**

natural gas

nitrogen   metal ores

hydrogen   salt water

the atmosphere

[2]

[Total 3 marks]

2 Dynamic equilibrium can occur in reversible reactions.

a) Compare the rates of the forwards and backwards reactions at dynamic equilibrium.
State how this affects the concentrations of reactants and products present at dynamic equilibrium.

....

....

[2]

b) Dynamic equilibrium can only be reached in a closed system.
Explain what is meant by a 'closed system'.

....

....

[1]

c) At equilibrium, a reaction is going in the forwards direction.
Give **one** factor that could be changed in order to change the direction of the reaction.

....

[1]

[Total 4 marks]

Exam Practice Tip

If there are more products than reactants at equilibrium, the reaction is going in the forwards direction. If there are more reactants than products, it's going in the backwards direction. But remember, the forward and backward reactions are going at the same rate — the amounts of products and reactants don't change.

Group 1 — Alkali Metals

1   The alkali metals are found in Group 1 of the periodic table.   *Grade 3-4*

a)   Which of the following statements is the **best** description of the alkali metals? Tick **one** box.

☐ **A** Soft metals with relatively high melting points.

☐ **B** Soft metals with relatively low melting points.

☐ **C** Hard metals with relatively high melting points.

☐ **D** Hard metals with relatively low melting points.

[1]

b)   Explain why the alkali metals react in similar ways.

....

[1]

[Total 2 marks]

2   A scientist adds small pieces of Group 1 metals to separate beakers of water.   *Grade 4-5*

a)   He first reacts a piece of sodium with some water. Complete the word equation for this reaction.

sodium + water → .... + ...

[2]

b)   State **one** observation that the scientist will make after he adds sodium to the water.

....

[1]

c)   He then reacts potassium with water. Potassium reacts more strongly than sodium with water.
Explain why.

....

....

....

....

[3]

d)   When added to water, the alkali metals readily react to form ionic compounds.
Explain why the ions of Group 1 metals have a charge of +1.

....

....

[2]

[Total 8 marks]

Group 7 — Halogens

1 Complete the passage about the Group 7 elements. Use the words in the box. **Grade 1-3**

| one | +1 | seven | halogens | halides | −1 | eight |

The Group 7 elements all have .... electrons in their outer shell.

They can react to form ions with a .... charge.

These ions are called ....

[Total 3 marks]

2 **Figure 1** shows a gas being tested. **Grade 3-4**

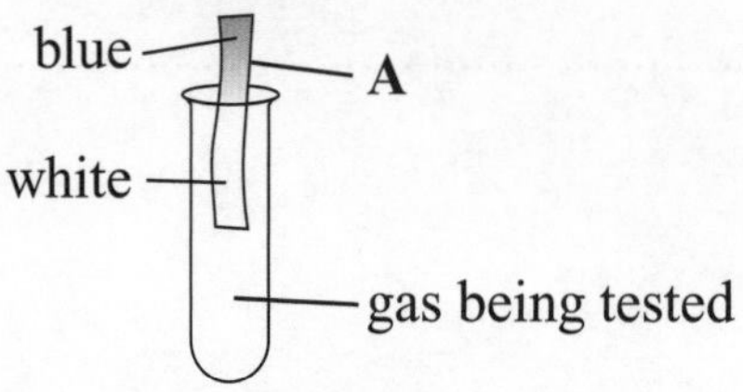

blue ———
A

white ———

gas being tested

Figure 1

a) Name the item labelled **A** in the diagram.

....

[1]

b) Suggest which halogen was present in the test tube.

....

[1]

[Total 2 marks]

3 Chlorine and bromine are both Group 7 elements. **Grade 4-5**

a) Which of these elements, chlorine or bromine, has a higher melting point?

....

[1]

b) Compare the chemical reactivity of chlorine and bromine. Explain your answer.

....

....

....

[3]

[Total 4 marks]

Exam Practice Tip

One of the most important things to learn about Group 7 elements is the trend you find in reactivity as you go down or up the group. And you need to be able to explain this trend using the electronic structure of the halogens. Smashing.

Reactions of Halogens

Tick the boxes to show whether the following statements are true or false.

	True	False
Halogens react with hydrogen to form hydrogen halides.	☐	☐
Hydrogen halides can dissolve in water.	☐	☐
Hydrogen halides form alkaline solutions.	☐	☐

1 Draw **one** line from each set of reactants to their product.

Reactants

bromine + lithium

iodine + hydrogen

bromine + hydrogen

Product

lithium iodide

hydrogen iodide

lithium bromide

hydrogen bromide

[Total 3 marks]

2 Halogens and halide salts can take part in halogen displacement reactions.

a) Describe what is meant by a displacement reaction.

....

[1]

b) **Figure 1** shows some experiments between halogens and halide solutions.
Place a tick (✓) in **one** box of each row to show whether or not a reaction will take place.

Halogen Water	Halide Solution	Reaction	No Reaction
chlorine water	potassium bromide		
iodine water	potassium bromide		
bromine water	potassium chloride		
chlorine water	potassium iodide		

Figure 1

[4]

[Total 5 marks]

Section 14 — Groups in the Periodic Table

108

3   The halogens can react with metals to form metal halide salts.   Grade 4-5

a) Name the metal halide salt that will be formed when the following pairs of elements react.

   i) Bromine and sodium.

   ....
   [1]

   ii) Iodine and potassium.

   ....
   [1]

b) When chlorine gas (Cl_2) reacts with lithium, the salt lithium chloride, LiCl, is formed. Write the balanced symbol equation for this reaction.

   ....
   [2]

c) Chlorine can also react with magnesium to form magnesium chloride. Suggest what product would be formed in a reaction between bromine and magnesium. Give a reason for your answer.

   Product: ....

   Reason: ....

   ....
   [2]

   [Total 6 marks]

4   A student adds an unknown sample of halogen water to three different halide solutions. **Figure 2** shows the results of each experiment.   Grade 4-5

Addition of halogen water to:		
Sodium chloride solution	**Sodium bromide solution**	**Sodium iodide solution**
no reaction	solution turns orange	solution turns brown

Figure 2

a) Which halogen was added to each of the halide solutions? Tick **one** box.

   ☐ **A** bromine   ☐ **B** iodine   ☐ **C** chlorine   ☐ **D** astatine
   [1]

b) Explain your answer to part a).

   ....

   ....
   [2]

c) Complete the word equation for the reaction that would take place between chlorine water and sodium astatide solution.

   chlorine + sodium astatide → .... + ...
   [2]

   [Total 5 marks]

Section 14 — Groups in the Periodic Table

Group 0 — Noble Gases

1   The Group 0 elements have similar properties.

a)   Describe the state of the Group 0 elements at room temperature.

....
[1]

b)   Some light bulbs are filled with argon to stop parts of the light bulb from burning away.
Argon is used because it is unreactive. Explain why argon is unreactive.

....
[1]

[Total 2 marks]

2   Group 0 elements show trends in their properties.
Information about some of their properties is shown in **Figure 1**.

Element	Boiling Point / °C	Density / kg m^{-3}
Neon	−246	0.90
Argon	−186	
Krypton	−152	
Xenon	−108	5.90
Radon		

Figure 1

a)   Using the information in **Figure 1**, predict the boiling point of radon.

boiling point of radon = ... °C
[1]

b)   Group 0 elements show a trend in their densities.
Predict the densities of argon, krypton and radon.
Use numbers from the box below.

0.73	1.78	9.73	0.21	3.74

density of argon = ... kg m^{-3}

density of krypton = ... kg m^{-3}

density of radon = ... kg m^{-3}
[3]

[Total 4 marks]

Exam Practice Tip

Make sure you get lots of practice at questions like Q2, where you're given information about some of the elements in a group and asked to use it to predict something about another element in the group. They need careful thinking through.

Section 14 — Groups in the Periodic Table

Reaction Rates

1   A student carries out a reaction in a conical flask. She measures the time it takes for a gas to be produced. Under different conditions, the rate of the reaction changes.

Complete the sentences below. Use words from the box.

| more quickly | more slowly | in the same time |

If the rate is higher than the rate of the original reaction,

the gas will be produced ....

If the rate is lower than the rate of the original reaction,

the gas will be produced ....

[Total 2 marks]

2   A student is investigating the effect of temperature on the rate of the reaction between sodium thiosulfate and hydrochloric acid. The reaction forms a cloudy, yellow precipitate of sulfur. Her experimental set up is shown in **Figure 1**.

PRACTICAL

dilute hydrochloric acid

sodium thiosulfate

black mark

start

stop

yellow precipitate

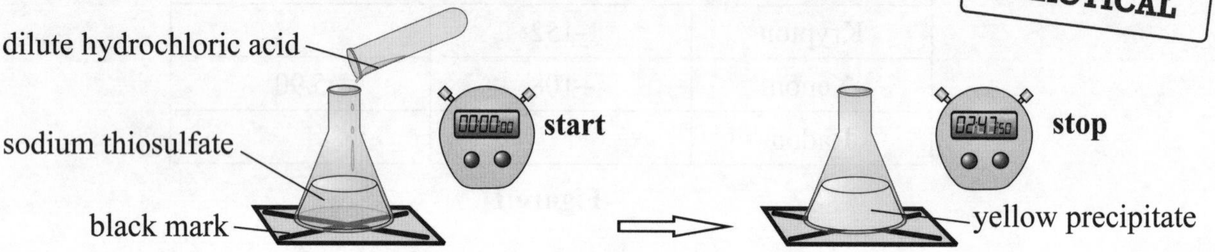

Figure 1

a) The first steps of the method are shown below:

> 1. Measure out 50 cm³ of sodium thiosulfate and 5 cm³ hydrochloric acid.
> 2. Use a water bath to gently heat both solutions to the desired temperature.
> 3. Mix the solutions in a conical flask.
> 4. Place the flask over a black mark on a piece of paper and start the stopwatch.

State the next step in this method.

....
[1]

b) What is the purpose of the black mark placed under the flask?

....
[1]

c) Another student repeats the same experiment. Why might he get a different result?

....
[1]

[Total 3 marks]

Rate Experiments Involving Gases

1   A certain reaction produces a gas product. Which piece of equipment below could be used to monitor the rate at which the gas is produced? Tick **one** box.

Grade 1-3

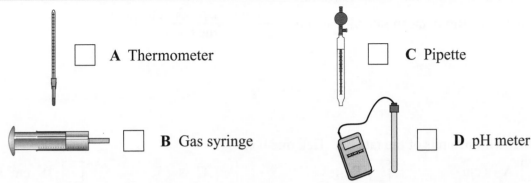

☐ **A** Thermometer

☐ **C** Pipette

☐ **B** Gas syringe

☐ **D** pH meter

[Total 1 mark]

2   A student measures the volume of gas produced by the reaction between sulfuric acid and marble chips. He repeats the experiment with two different concentrations of acid, **A** and **B**, using the same mass of marble chips. **Figure 1** shows his results.

Grade 4-5

		Time (s)							
		0	10	20	30	40	50	60	70
Volume of gas produced (cm³)	Concentration A	0	13	16	17	17	17	17	17
	Concentration B	0	6	9	12	14	16	17	17

Figure 1

a) State the concentration, **A** or **B**, which resulted in the fastest reaction.
Give a reason for your answer.

Concentration: ....

Reason: ....

....

[2]

b) **Figure 2** shows a graph of the results for concentration B. The student repeats the experiment with the same concentration of acid, but using powdered chalk with the same mass as the marble chips. The rate of the reaction increases. On **Figure 2**, sketch a curve for this experiment.

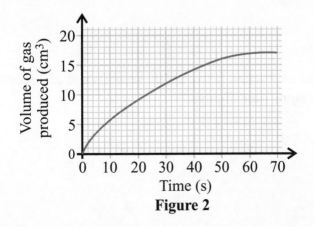

Figure 2

[2]

[Total 4 marks]

 ☐   ☐   ☐

Section 15 — Rates of Reaction and Energy Changes

Calculating Rates

1   In a reaction that lasted 125 seconds, 4.0 g of gas was produced.

   a) Calculate the mean rate of the reaction.

     Use the equation: mean rate of reaction $= \dfrac{\text{amount of product formed}}{\text{time taken}}$

     .... units

     [2]

   b) What will the units of the rate be? Tick **one** box.

     ☐ **A** $s\ cm^{-3}$ ☐ **B** $g\ s^{-1}$ ☐ **C** $s\ g^{-1}$ ☐ **D** $cm^{3}\ s^{-1}$

     [1]

     [Total 3 marks]

2   **Figure 1** shows the volume of hydrogen gas produced during a reaction between magnesium and hydrochloric acid.

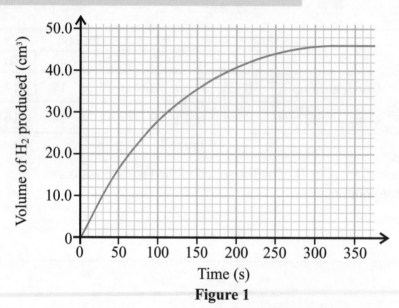

Figure 1

   a) Calculate the mean rate for the whole reaction. Give your answer to 3 significant figures.

     Use **Figure 1** and the equation: mean rate of reaction $= \dfrac{\text{amount of product formed}}{\text{time taken}}$

     .... $cm^{3}\ s^{-1}$

     [2]

   b) Calculate the mean rate of reaction between 100 seconds and 250 seconds.
     Give your answer to 3 significant figures.

     .... $cm^{3}\ s^{-1}$

     [4]

     [Total 6 marks]

3   The rate of a reaction was investigated by measuring the volume of gas produced at regular intervals. Part of the results are shown in **Figure 2**.

Time (s)	0	10	20	30	40	50
Volume of gas (cm³)	0.0	3.0	5.5	9.5	12.0	15.0

Figure 2

a) Plot the data in **Figure 2** on the axes below.

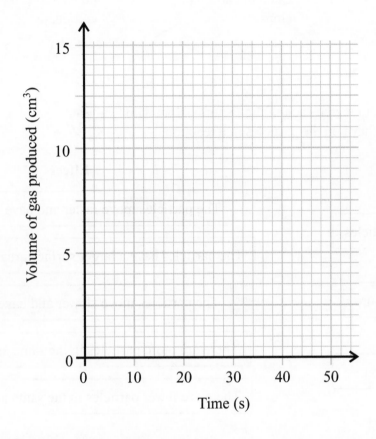

[2]

b) Calculate the gradient of your graph.

gradient = ...
[2]

c) What is the rate of this reaction? Include the units in your answer.

rate = ...
[1]

[Total 5 marks]

Exam Practice Tip

Plotting graphs can sometimes take a while, but make sure you take your time. It's easy to miss out a point or plot an x-value with the wrong y-value. You might be given a graph which doesn't have many values on the axis (like the graph's y-axis on this page). If so, feel free to add more values or markers to make it quicker and easier to plot your graph.

Section 15 — Rates of Reaction and Energy Changes

Collision Theory

A student reacts nitric acid with three different forms of calcium carbonate. All other variables are kept the same. Circle the condition that will result in the slowest rate of reaction.

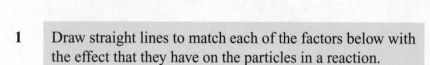

lump of calcium carbonate

calcium carbonate chips

powdered calcium carbonate

1   Draw straight lines to match each of the factors below with the effect that they have on the particles in a reaction.

Factor

using smaller particles

increasing pressure

increasing temperature

Effect

The particles move faster and have more energy.

The particles have a larger surface area to volume ratio.

The particles move slower and have less energy.

There are more particles in the same amount of space.

There are fewer particles in the same amount of space.

[Total 3 marks]

2   A student is investigating the effect of concentration of acid on the reaction between zinc and hydrochloric acid.

a) Why does increasing the concentration of acid mean that there are more collisions between the particles?

....

....

....

[2]

b) What is the name given to the minimum amount of energy which particles must have if they are to react when they collide?

....

[1]

[Total 3 marks]

Section 15 — Rates of Reaction and Energy Changes

Catalysts

1 Which of the following statements about catalysts is true? Tick **one** box. (Grade 1-3)

- [ ] **A** Catalysts get used up in a reaction.
- [ ] **B** Catalysts decrease the rate of a reaction.
- [ ] **C** Catalysts change the products of the reaction.
- [ ] **D** Catalysts provide a different reaction pathway.

[Total 1 mark]

2 **Figure 1** shows the reaction profiles for a reaction carried out with and without a catalyst. (Grade 3-4)

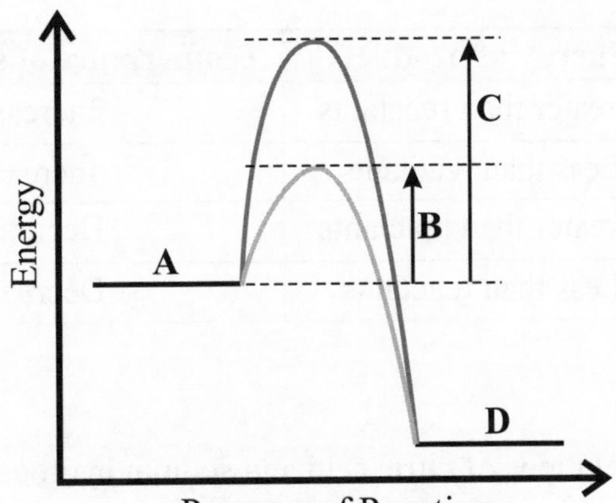

Figure 1

a) i) Which label, **A–D**, shows the level of energy of the reactants?

....

[1]

ii) Which label, **A–D**, shows the activation energy needed
for the reaction carried out without a catalyst?

....

[1]

b) Describe what happens to the amount of catalyst in a
reaction mixture over the course of a reaction.

....

[1]

c) Enzymes are biological catalysts. Give **one** example of a use of enzymes as catalysts.

....

[1]

[Total 4 marks]

Section 15 — Rates of Reaction and Energy Changes

Endothermic and Exothermic Reactions

Warm-Up

Complete the following definition of an exothermic reaction.
Use words from the box.

| takes in | gives out | rise | fall |

An exothermic reaction is one that .... energy.

This is shown by a .... in the temperature of the surroundings.

1   Which of the following energy changes describes an exothermic reaction? Tick **one** box.   (Grade 3-4)

	Energy of products	Temperature of surroundings
☐ A	Greater than reactants	Increases
☐ B	Less than reactants	Increases
☐ C	Greater than reactants	Decreases
☐ D	Less than reactants	Decreases

[Total 1 mark]

2   During a reaction between solutions of citric acid and sodium hydrogen carbonate,   (Grade 4-5)
the temperature of the surroundings went down.

a) Is this reaction exothermic or endothermic? Give a reason for your answer.

    ....

    [2]

b) In this reaction, the products are at a higher energy than the reactants.
Sketch a reaction profile for this reaction on the axes below.
Label the reactants and products.

Energy

Progress of reaction

[2]

[Total 4 marks]

Exam Practice Tip

The 'en' in 'endothermic' sounds like 'in', and the 'do' is the start of 'down'. So endothermic reactions take energy <u>in</u> from
the surroundings, and make the temperature of the surroundings go <u>down</u>. Exothermic reactions do the opposite.

Bond Energies and Activation Energy

1 Energy changes take place when bonds are broken and formed during chemical reactions. **Grade 4-5**

Which of the following statements is true? Tick **one** box.

☐ **A** During exothermic reactions, the energy used to break bonds is greater than the energy released by forming them.

☐ **B** During endothermic reactions, the energy released by breaking bonds is less than the energy taken in to form them.

☐ **C** During exothermic reactions, the energy used to break bonds is less than the energy released by forming them.

☐ **D** During endothermic reactions, the energy used to break bonds is less than the energy released by forming them.

[Total 1 mark]

2 **Figure 1** shows the reaction profile for a reaction. **Grade 4-5**

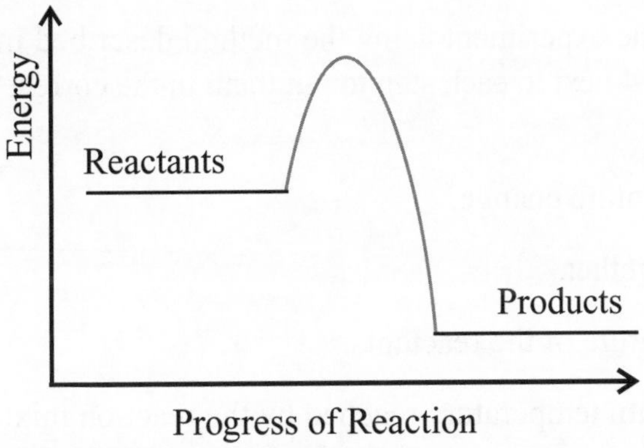

Figure 1

a) What type of reaction is represented by **Figure 1**?

....

[1]

b) i) Draw an arrow and label it to show the overall energy change on **Figure 1**.

[1]

ii) Draw an arrow and label it to show the activation energy on **Figure 1**.

[1]

c) Define the term 'activation energy'.

....

....

[1]

[Total 4 marks]

Section 15 — Rates of Reaction and Energy Changes

Measuring Temperature Changes

1   A student investigated the temperature change of the reaction between sodium hydroxide and hydrochloric acid. The student set up the equipment as shown in **Figure 1**.

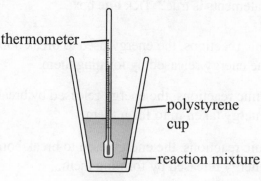

thermometer

polystyrene cup

reaction mixture

Figure 1

a) Suggest **one** way the student should change the set-up shown in **Figure 1** in order to make the results more accurate. Give a reason for your answer.

Change: ....

Reason: ....

[2]

b) The student carried out the experiment using the method described in the steps below. Write a number 1, 2, 3 or 4 next to each step to put them in the correct order.

Step	**Step number**
Calculate the temperature change.	....
Mix the reactants together.	....
Measure the temperature of the reactants.	....
Measure the maximum temperature reached by the reaction mixture.	....

[2]

c) The results of the experiment are shown in **Figure 2**.

Initial Temperature (°C)	Final Temperature (°C)
18	31

Figure 2

Calculate the temperature change of the reaction.

Temperature change = ... °C

[1]

d) The student repeated the experiment a number of times using a different concentration of acid each time. State the independent and dependent variables in this experiment.

Independent: ....

Dependent: ....

[2]

[Total 7 marks]

Section 15 — Rates of Reaction and Energy Changes

Fractional Distillation

Warm-Up

Draw a line to match each of the following fractions of crude oil with one of its main uses.

Bitumen		Fuel for aircraft
Diesel		Surfacing roads and roofs
Kerosene		Fuel for cars and trains

1   **Figure 1** shows a fractionating column.
They are used in the fractional distillation of crude oil.

Grade 1-3

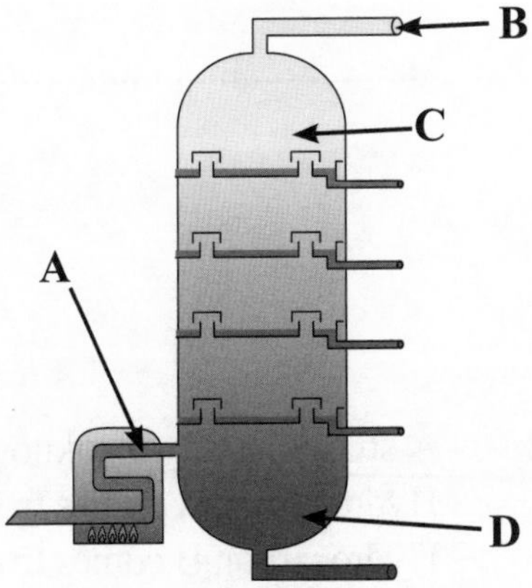

a) Where does crude oil enter the fractionating column?
Tick **one** box.

☐ A   ☐ B   ☐ C   ☐ D

[1]

b) Which is the hottest part of the fractionating column?
Tick **one** box.

☐ A   ☐ B   ☐ C   ☐ D

[1]

c) Where do the shortest hydrocarbons leave the fractionating column?
Tick **one** box.

☐ A   ☐ B   ☐ C   ☐ D

Figure 1

[1]

[Total 3 marks]

2   Crude oil is a complex mixture of hydrocarbons.

Grade 3-4

a) What is the most common type of hydrocarbon found in crude oil?

....

[1]

b) Crude oil is a finite resource. What does this mean?

....

[1]

[Total 2 marks]

Exam Practice Tip

You're expected to remember the names and main uses of the different crude oil fractions (gases, petrol, kerosene, diesel oil, fuel oil and bitumen). In general, the lighter fractions (petrol, kerosene) are used as fuels in lighter vehicles (like cars) and heavier fractions (diesel and fuel oils) are used for heavier tasks (like fuelling power stations).

 ☐   ☐   ☐

Hydrocarbons

1 A homologous series is the name given to a family of molecules.
Crude oil is a mixture of different homologous series of hydrocarbons.

Grade
3-4

a) What is a hydrocarbon?

....

[2]

b) Molecular formulas of neighbouring hydrocarbons in a homologous series differ by the same amount.
State the formula of the unit that they differ by.

....

[1]

c) What effect does increasing chain length have on the viscosity of hydrocarbons in a homologous series?

....

[1]

[Total 4 marks]

2 A student has two unknown hydrocarbons, A and B.
Hydrocarbon A comes from the bitumen fraction of crude oil.
Hydrocarbon B comes from the kerosene fraction.
Bitumen contains hydrocarbons with much longer chain lengths than kerosene.

Grade
4-5

a) The student attempts to ignite hydrocarbons A and B using a spark.
Suggest predictions for what will happen to **each** hydrocarbon.

Hydrocarbon A: ....

Hydrocarbon B: ....

[2]

b) Explain which hydrocarbon, A or B, has the highest boiling point.

....

....

[1]

[Total 3 marks]

Exam Practice Tip

Make sure you can remember the elements that are in a hydrocarbon. They're there in the name — 'hydro' means
there's hydrogen, and 'carbon' means there's... well... carbon. The hydrocarbons are a hard club to get into. If a molecule
contains even one atom of any other element, then it won't be a hydrocarbon. How very mean.

Combustion of Fuels

1 Many hydrocarbons are used as fuels. [Grade 3-4]

a) Methane is a non-renewable fossil fuel that is found in natural gas.
Give **one** example of a non-renewable fuel obtained from crude oil.

....
[1]

b) Combustion is the process of burning a fuel in air.
Describe the energy change that takes place when a fuel combusts.

....
[1]

c) Complete combustion occurs when a hydrocarbon fuel is burned in an excess of oxygen.
Complete the equation given below for complete combustion.

hydrocarbon + oxygen → .... + ...
[1]

d) When complete combustion cannot take place, incomplete combustion occurs.
Under what condition does incomplete combustion take place?

....
[1]

e) State the products, other than water and carbon dioxide, that can form during incomplete combustion.

....
[1]

[Total 5 marks]

2 Combustion of fuel in cars can cause air pollution. [Grade 4-5]

a) Fuel combustion can produce tiny particles of carbon.
What impact do these particles have on human health?

....
[1]

b) Combustion of fuels can also produce a toxic gas that can stop oxygen from getting to the brain.
Name the gas and explain how it could stop oxygen from reaching the brain.

Name: ....

Explanation: ....

....
[3]

[Total 4 marks]

Pollutants

1 Draw **one** line from each pollutant to show how it's formed.

Pollutant	How Pollutant is Formed

Incomplete combustion of hydrocarbons.

sulfur dioxide

Reaction of gases in the air caused
by the heat of burning fossil fuels.

nitrogen oxides

Combustion of fossil fuels that contain sulfur impurities.

[Total 2 marks]

2 Some of the pollutants that are released when fuels burn can cause acid rain. (Grade 3-4)

a) Name **one** pollutant that can lead to acid rain.

....

[1]

b) State **two** ways in which acid rain can be damaging.

....

....

[2]

[Total 3 marks]

3 Combustion of fuel in cars is a major contributor to air pollution. (Grade 4-5)

a) Nitrogen oxides can be formed from the combustion of fuels in cars.
Give **two** problems caused by nitrogen oxides in the environment.

....

....

[2]

b) Hydrogen gas can also be used as a fuel to power cars.

i) Give **two** advantages of using hydrogen as a fuel in cars, rather than petrol.

1: ....

2: ....

[2]

ii) Give **two** disadvantages of using hydrogen as a fuel in cars, rather than petrol.

1: ....

2: ....

[2]

[Total 6 marks]

Cracking

1   Some fractions of crude oil are processed by cracking.

a)   Define the term 'cracking'.

....
[1]

b)   Name **two** types of hydrocarbons that are produced as a result of cracking.

1 ....   2 ....
[2]

c)   Why are long-chain hydrocarbons often processed by cracking?

....
[1]

[Total 4 marks]

2   **Figure 1** shows the approximate percentage of each hydrocarbon fraction produced by an oil refinery, and the demand for each fraction.

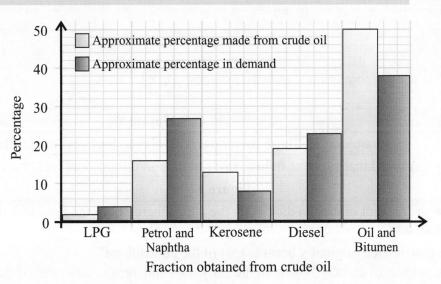

Figure 1

Look at **Figure 1**. Tick the correct box in each row of the table to show whether the statements are true or false.

Statement	True	False
The LPG fraction can be cracked to supply more petrol.		
The demand for petrol and naphtha is greater than the amount made by the refinery.		
The demand for diesel can be met by cracking oil and bitumen.		
More kerosene is produced than there is demand for.		

[Total 4 marks]

Section 16 — Fuels and Earth Science

The Atmosphere

Warm-Up

Write the numbers 1-4 in the boxes below to put the events in the order in which they happened.

Oxygen levels began to rise. ☐   The oceans formed. ☐

The early atmosphere formed. ☐   Plants evolved. ☐

1   The composition of gases in the atmosphere has changed during Earth's history.   **Grade 3-4**

a) The level of oxygen in the atmosphere has increased over Earth's history. Give a reason for this change.

....

[1]

b) Describe the chemical test for oxygen.

....

[1]

c) The early Earth was much hotter than today.
Describe what happened to the water vapour in the atmosphere as the Earth cooled.

....

[1]

[Total 3 marks]

2*   **Figure 1** shows some information about two fossils.   **Grade 4-5**

Age (years)	Description
950 000 000	Cyanobacteria. These bacteria can survive in high levels of carbon dioxide.
295 000 000	A lizard that survives in low levels of carbon dioxide and higher levels of oxygen.

Figure 1

Describe how the amount of carbon dioxide in the atmosphere got to the level that it is at today.
Include ideas about:

* How carbon dioxide originally became part of the atmosphere.
* How the amount of carbon dioxide in the early atmosphere was different to how it is today.
* Reasons why the amount of atmospheric carbon dioxide has changed.
* Whether the information in **Figure 1** supports your answer.

....

....

....

....

....

....

....

[Total 6 marks]

Climate Change And The Greenhouse Effect

1 An increase in the human population has been linked to climate change. (Grade 3-4)

a) What change does an increasing population have on the energy demand of the planet?
Give **one** example of an activity that is responsible for this change.

Change: ....

Example: ....

[2]

b) Action can be taken on climate change at many different levels.
Complete the table by putting a tick in the box that shows the
best scale of organisation for carrying out that action.
The first row has been completed for you.

Action	Small Business	Government
Putting a tax on light bulbs that use lots of energy		✓
Building wind turbines		
Capturing carbon dioxide and storing it underground		
Printing on recycled paper		
Starting a car share scheme		

[4]

[Total 6 marks]

2 Most scientists believe that human activity is causing climate change. (Grade 3-4)

a) What has the general change in global temperatures been over the past 100 years?

....

[1]

b) Give **two** examples of climate change that could be caused by changing global temperatures.

1: ....

2: ....

[2]

c) Give **one** possible reason for the change in temperature.

....

[1]

[Total 4 marks]

3 Greenhouse gases in the atmosphere help maintain life on Earth.

a) Give **two** examples of greenhouses gases.

....

[1]

b) Use the words in the box below to complete the paragraph describing the greenhouse effect.

thermal	absorbed	cools	radiation	reflected	warms

The sun gives out ....

The Earth reflects this as .... radiation.

This radiation is .... by greenhouse gases and then given out in all directions.

Some heads back to Earth and .... the Earth's surface.

[4]

[Total 5 marks]

4 **Figure 1** shows how global carbon dioxide concentration has changed over time.

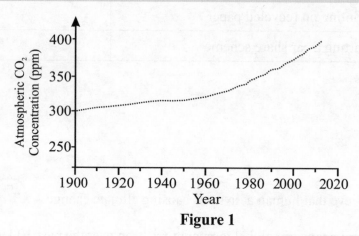

Figure 1

a) Describe how carbon dioxide levels have changed since 1900.

....

[1]

b) State **one** man-made cause of the change in carbon dioxide in the atmosphere.

....

[1]

c) Give **two** reasons why it may be less accurate to extend the graph further back in time than 1900.

1: ....

2: ....

[2]

[Total 4 marks]

Section 16 — Fuels and Earth Science

Distance, Displacement, Speed and Velocity

1 A quantity can be either a scalar or a vector.
Compare and contrast scalar and vector quantities.

Grade 3-4

....

....

[Total 2 marks]

2 **Figure 1** shows the path taken by a football kicked by a child. When it is kicked at point A, the ball moves horizontally to the right until it hits a vertical wall at point B. The ball then bounces back horizontally to the left and comes to rest at point C.

Grade 3-4

Figure 1

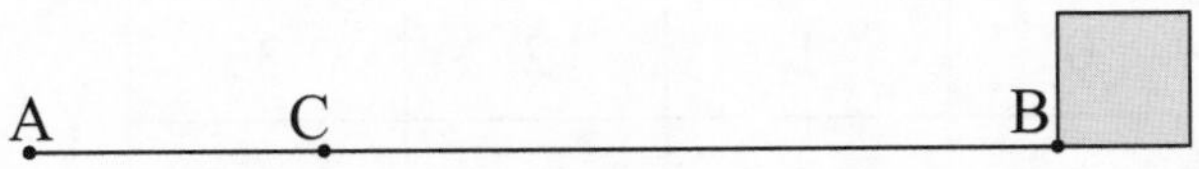

Scale 1 cm = 1 m

A   C   B

a) Determine the total distance travelled by the ball as it moves from A to B.

Distance = ... m

[1]

b) Calculate the total distance travelled by the ball.

Distance = ... m

[1]

c) Determine the magnitude of the displacement of the ball after it has come to rest.

Displacement = ... m

[1]

[Total 3 marks]

3 A man walks 7 km to his work place. Estimate how long his journey takes, using your knowledge of typical speeds.

Grade 4-5

Use the equation:

$$\text{average speed} = \text{distance} \div \text{time}$$

Time taken = ... s

[Total 4 marks]

Acceleration

Warm-Up

Draw one line from each object to the typical acceleration for that object.

A sprinter starting a race	10 m/s²
A falling object	2×10^5 m/s²
A bullet shot from a gun	1.5 m/s²

1 **Figure 1** shows how the velocity of a car changes with time as it accelerates uniformly. Grade 3-4

Figure 1

Time (s)	0	1	2	3
Velocity (m/s)	0	4	8	12

Calculate the acceleration of the car. Use the equation:

acceleration = change in velocity ÷ time taken

Acceleration = ... m/s^2

[Total 3 marks]

2 Three cars, A, B and C, are travelling at 25 m/s. As they approach a turning, each of them slows down to 15 m/s. Car A takes 10 s to slow down. Car B takes 7 s to slow down. Car C takes 5 s to slow down. Grade 3-4

State and explain which car has the largest deceleration.

....

....

[Total 2 marks]

3 A train is travelling at 18 m/s. It accelerates uniformly to a speed of 32 m/s over a distance of 350 m. Calculate the acceleration of the train over this distance. Use an equation from the Equations List. Grade 4-5

Acceleration = ... m/s^2

[Total 3 marks]

Distance/Time Graphs

1 A boat is being rowed along a straight canal. Some students time how long it takes the boat to pass markers spaced 100 metres apart. **Figure 1** shows their results.

Figure 1

Distance (m)	0	100	200	300	400	500
Time (s)	0	85	170	255	340	425

Figure 2

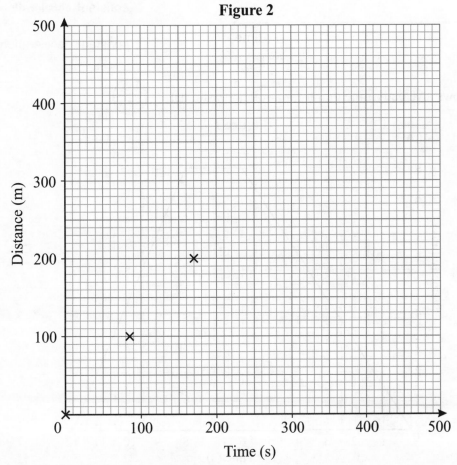

Time (s)

a) Complete the distance-time graph in **Figure 2** using the results in **Figure 1**.

[2]

b) Using the graph in **Figure 2**, estimate how far the boat travelled in 300 s.

Distance = ... m

[1]

c) Using the graph in **Figure 2**, estimate how long it took the boat to travel 250 m.

Time = ... s

[1]

d) Describe the boat's speed during the first 500 m of its journey.

....

[1]

[Total 5 marks]

Section 17 — Motion, Forces and Conservation of Energy

Velocity/Time Graphs

Use two of the phrases from the list below to correctly label the velocity/time graph.

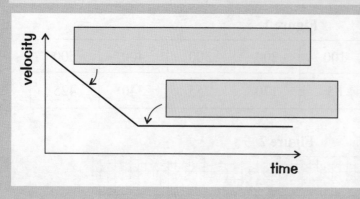

decreasing deceleration

steady speed

decreasing acceleration

constant acceleration

constant deceleration

1 **Figure 1** shows a velocity/time graph for a roller coaster car.

Figure 1

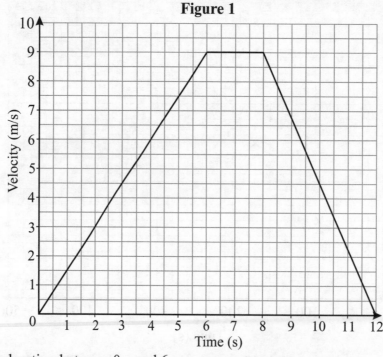

Time (s)

a) The car is accelerating between 0 s and 6 s.
Using the graph in **Figure 1**, calculate the acceleration for the car between 0 s and 6 s.

Acceleration = ... m/s²

[3]

b) Calculate the distance travelled by the car while it is travelling at a constant speed.

Distance travelled = ... m

[3]

[Total 6 marks]

Section 17 — Motion, Forces and Conservation of Energy

Weight

Warm-Up

State whether each of the following statements are true or false.

1) Weight is a force caused by gravity. _____

2) The weight of an object is the same as its mass. _____

3) Weight can be measured using a voltmeter. _____

1 Which of the following statements correctly describes the relationship between gravitational field strength and the weight of an object? Tick **one** box.

(Grade 1-3)

☐ **A** The larger the gravitational field strength, the smaller the weight.

☐ **B** The larger the gravitational field strength, the larger the weight.

☐ **C** Gravitational field strength and weight are the same thing.

☐ **D** There is no relationship between gravitational field strength and weight.

[Total 1 mark]

2 The Opportunity rover is a 185 kg robot. It was made on Earth and sent to the surface of the planet Mars.

(Grade 4-5)

a) State the equation that links weight, mass and gravitational field strength.

....
[1]

b) Calculate the weight of Opportunity when it was on Earth.
(The gravitational field strength on the surface of Earth = 10 N/kg.)

Weight = ... N
[2]

c) The weight of Opportunity on Mars is 703 N.
Calculate the gravitational field strength on the surface of Mars.

Gravitational field strength = ... N/kg
[3]

[Total 6 marks]

Exam Practice Tip

If you're struggling to remember an equation, looking at the units of the values you've been given might help you.
If the units include a slash (like N/kg), it shows that something must be divided by something else to get that value.

    Section 17 — Motion, Forces and Conservation of Energy

Resultant Force and Newton's First Law

1 **Figure 1** shows the forces acting on four runners. Tick the box
under the runner who has a non-zero resultant force acting on them.

Figure 1

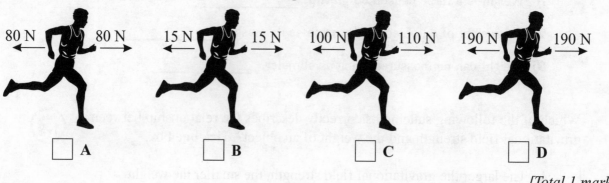

80 N ← → 80 N   15 N ← → 15 N   100 N ← → 110 N   190 N ← → 190 N

☐ A   ☐ B   ☐ C   ☐ D

[Total 1 mark]

2 Complete the statement of Newton's First Law using phrases from the box below.

increase	gravitational	decrease	stay the same	resultant

Newton's First Law states that if the .... force acting

on a moving object is zero, the velocity of the object will ....

If the force is non-zero and acts in the opposite direction to the movement of the object,

the velocity of the object will ....

[Total 3 marks]

3 A van is at rest on a hill.

a) State and explain the size of the resultant force acting on the van.

    ....

    ....

    ....

    [2]

b) The van accelerates up the hill until it reaches a speed of 25 m/s.
It then remains travelling at 25 m/s.
Describe how the resultant force acting on the van changes during this time.

    ....

    ....

    ....

    [2]

    [Total 4 marks]

Newton's Second Law

1   **Figure 1** shows an accelerating motorbike. It shows the resultant force acting on the motorbike. The motorbike and rider have a combined mass of 400 kg.

Figure 1

2400 N

a)   State the equation that links force, mass and acceleration.

....

[1]

b)   Calculate the acceleration of the motorbike.

Acceleration = ... m/s^2

[3]

[Total 4 marks]

2*   If a driver sees a hazard on the road, they may have to apply a large braking force to avoid hitting the hazard. If they do this while travelling at high speed, it can be very dangerous.

Explain how applying a large braking force while travelling at a high speed can be dangerous. You should refer to Newton's Second Law in your answer.

....

....

....

....

....

....

....

....

....

....

....

[Total 6 marks]

         Section 17 — Motion, Forces and Conservation of Energy

Investigating Motion

1   **Figure 1** shows the equipment used by a student to investigate how changing the force on a trolley changes its acceleration.

Figure 1

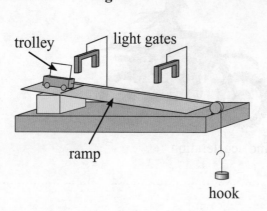

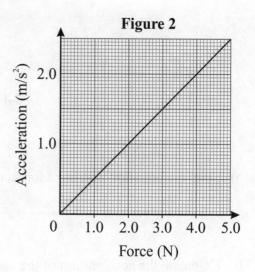

The student changes the force on the trolley by moving a mass from the trolley to the hook. The acceleration of the trolley for different forces is calculated.

a) Describe how the light gates can be used to find the acceleration of the trolley.

    ....

    ....

    ....
                                                                                                                        [3]

Figure 2 is a graph of acceleration against force for the trolley.

b) Give **one** conclusion that can be made from **Figure 2**.

    ....

    ....
                                                                                                                        [1]

c) Using **Figure 2**, calculate the mass being accelerated.
    Use the equation:

    $$\text{force} = \text{mass} \times \text{acceleration}$$

                                                                                        Mass = ... kg
                                                                                                                        [3]

d) The mass on the hook was kept the same. 50 g of mass was added to the trolley.
    State the effect this will have on the acceleration of the trolley.

    ....
                                                                                                                        [1]

                                                                                                            [Total 8 marks]

Section 17 — Motion, Forces and Conservation of Energy

Newton's Third Law

Warm-Up

Which of the following is Newton's Third Law? Tick **one** box.

The acceleration of an object depends on the resultant force on the object. ☐

When two objects interact, they exert equal and opposite forces on each other. ☐

If an object at rest is acted on by a zero resultant force, it will not start moving. ☐

1 **Figure 1** shows skater A pushing on skater B with a force of 100 N. Using Newton's Third Law, what force does skater B exert on skater A? Tick **one** box.

Grade 1-3

Figure 1

☐ **A** 50 N

☐ **B** 150 N

☐ **C** 200 N

☐ **D** 100 N

[Total 1 mark]

2 **Figure 2** shows the forces acting on a gymnast balancing on two beams. The 320 N forces are normal contact forces, and the 640 N force is his weight. The gymnast is in equilibrium.

Figure 2

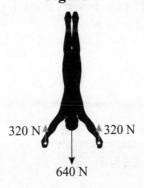

320 N   320 N

640 N

a) State what is meant when an object is said to be in equilibrium.

....

[1]

b) State the size of the attractive force exerted on the Earth by the gymnast.

Force = ... N

[1]

[Total 2 marks]

Exam Practice Tip

Be careful with Newton's Third Law. A pair of forces produced by Newton's Third Law will always be the same type of force and will always act on different objects. If both forces are acting on the same object, it's not Newton's Third Law.

   Section 17 — Motion, Forces and Conservation of Energy

Stopping Distances

1   Which of the following is the correct equation for stopping distance? Tick **one** box.   *Grade 1-3*

  ☐ **A**   stopping distance = braking distance + thinking distance

  ☐ **B**   stopping distance = braking distance – thinking distance

  ☐ **C**   stopping distance = braking distance × thinking distance

  ☐ **D**   stopping distance = braking distance ÷ thinking distance

[Total 1 mark]

2   The stopping distance of a vehicle depends on the driver's thinking distance.   *Grade 3-4*

a)   State what is meant by the term 'thinking distance'.

....

[1]

b)   State and explain the effect drinking alcohol would have on a driver's thinking distance.

....

....

[2]

c)   State **one** other factor which can affect a driver's thinking distance.

....

[1]

[Total 4 marks]

3   A car is travelling along a flat road and has to stop in an emergency. Its braking distance is 18 m.   *Grade 3-4*

a)   State what is meant by the term 'braking distance'.

....

[1]

b)   The car travels down the same road the next day. There is ice on the road.
Explain how the braking distance of the car would be affected by the change in conditions.

....

....

....

[2]

[Total 3 marks]

Section 17 — Motion, Forces and Conservation of Energy   ☐   ☐   ☐

Reaction Times

1   A teacher tests the reaction times of three of her students.
She measures how far a ruler vertically falls before the student catches it.

a) Explain why it would not be suitable to use a stopwatch to measure a student's reaction time.

....
[1]

Figure 1 shows the teacher's results.
The values in the table show the distance the ruler falls in centimetres during each attempt.

Figure 1

	Attempt 1 (cm)	Attempt 2 (cm)	Attempt 3 (cm)	Average (cm)
Student A	27.0	27.1	26.9	27.0
Student B	28.4	28.2	28.3	28.3
Student C	26.5	27.0	26.0	26.5

b) State and explain which student has the fastest average reaction time.

....

....
[2]

c) Give **two** ways the teacher could make the experiment a fair test.

1. ....

2. ....
[2]

d) The teacher repeats the experiment.
This time, she has someone talk to each student while they are being tested.
Describe how you would expect this to affect the reaction times of the students.

....
[1]

e) A fourth student, Student D, tests his reaction time using the same method as the teacher.
He calculates his reaction time as 4.5 s.
Explain how you know Student D has made an error in his experiment.

....

....
[1]

[Total 7 marks]

Section 17 — Motion, Forces and Conservation of Energy

Energy Stores and Conservation of Energy

1 Which statement about energy is **true**? Tick **one** box. *(Grade 1-3)*

☐ **A** Energy can be created and destroyed.

☐ **B** Energy can be created but not destroyed.

☐ **C** Energy can be destroyed but not created.

☐ **D** Energy cannot be created or destroyed.

[Total 1 mark]

2 Draw **one** straight line from each object to the energy store that energy is being transferred **from**. *(Grade 1-3)*

Object   **Energy store**

A car slowing down without braking.   chemical energy store

A mug of hot tea cooling down.   thermal energy store

A stretched spring returning to its original shape. elastic potential energy store

A battery in a circuit.   kinetic energy store

[Total 3 marks]

3 A hot spoon is sealed inside a thermally-insulated flask full of cold water. This is a closed system. *(Grade 3-4)*

a) Describe a closed system in terms of energy transfers.

....

....

[1]

b) Describe **one** energy transfer that occurs within the closed system.

....

....

[2]

[Total 3 marks]

Exam Practice Tip

In the exams, you might be given a situation and be asked to describe which stores energy is transferred to and from. If you're unsure what energy stores are involved in a transfer, look for clues in the question. For example, if something is lifted above the ground, energy must have been transferred to its gravitational potential energy store.

Section 17 — Motion, Forces and Conservation of Energy

Energy Transfers

A ball is rolling along the ground. Friction causes it to slow down and eventually stop.
Fill in the gap in the energy transfer diagram using a word given below.

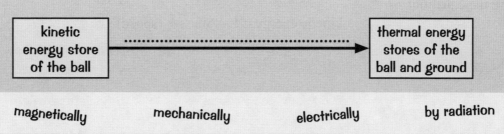

| kinetic energy store of the ball | ....> | thermal energy stores of the ball and ground |

magnetically   mechanically   electrically   by radiation

---

1 Use phrases from the box below to complete the passage. Grade 3-4

| thermal | kinetic | electrically | mechanically | by heating |

An electric kettle is used to heat some water. When the kettle is on, energy is transferred

.... to the thermal energy store of the kettle's heating element.

The energy is then transferred to the water ....

The energy is transferred to the water's .... energy store.

[Total 3 marks]

---

2 A child slides down a snowy hill on a sledge. Grade 4-5

a) Describe the main energy transfer that occurs as the sledge travels down the hill.
   You may assume there is no friction between the snow and the sledge.

   ....

   ....

   ....

   [3]

b) At the bottom of the hill, the sledge passes onto a flat section of grass.
   The sledge slows down due to friction.
   Describe the energy transfers that occur as the sledge slows down.

   ....

   ....

   ....

   ....

   [3]

   [Total 6 marks]

            Section 17 — Motion, Forces and Conservation of Energy

Kinetic and Potential Energy Stores

1   A cyclist is travelling along a road at 5.0 m/s. The total energy in the kinetic energy stores of the cyclist and the bike is 1.1 kJ.

Calculate the total mass of the cyclist and bike.
Use the equation:

$$\text{kinetic energy} = \tfrac{1}{2} \times \text{mass} \times (\text{speed})^2$$

Mass = ... kg

[Total 3 marks]

2   A girl kicks a ball resting on the ground into the air.
The ball reaches a height of 2.0 m. The ball has a mass of 0.50 kg.
Gravitational field strength = 10 N/kg.

a) State the equation that links change in gravitational potential energy, mass, gravitational field strength and change in vertical height.

....

[1]

b) Calculate the energy transferred to the ball's gravitational potential energy store.

Energy = ... J

[2]

c) The ball falls back down to the ground. All of the energy stored in the ball's gravitational potential energy store is transferred to its kinetic energy store.
Calculate the speed of the ball when it hits the ground.
Give your answer to 2 significant figures.

Speed = ... m/s

[3]

[Total 6 marks]

Exam Practice Tip

Be careful with equations involving squared values (^{2}), like the equation for kinetic energy above. Make sure you remember to square the value (multiply it by itself) when you type it out in your calculator. It might be helpful to write it out in full so you don't forget. For example: kinetic energy = ½ × mass × speed × speed.

Section 17 — Motion, Forces and Conservation of Energy

Efficiency

1 **Figure 1** shows how much energy is usefully transferred by three different desk fans, A, B and C, during 1 hour of use. Each desk fan is supplied with the same amount of energy from the mains supply.

Figure 1

	Desk Fan A	Desk Fan B	Desk Fan C
Energy transferred usefully (J)	88 000	85 000	86 000

a) State and explain which desk fan is the most efficient.

....

....

[2]

b) Friction acts between the moving parts of each desk fan.
Describe **one** energy transfer that occurs within a desk fan that is not useful.

....

....

....

[3]

[Total 5 marks]

2 A mobile phone battery has an efficiency of 72%. After being fully charged, the battery transfers 18 000 J of energy usefully before it needs to be charged again.

a) State the equation that links efficiency, useful energy transferred by the device, and total energy supplied to the device.

....

[1]

b) Calculate the total energy supplied to the battery to fully charge it.

Total energy supplied = ... J

[3]

[Total 4 marks]

Exam Practice Tip

Remember, efficiency can be given either as a decimal or as a percentage. Make sure you know how to convert between the two forms. If you're substituting it into an equation, you'll usually need the efficiency to be a decimal.

     Section 17 — Motion, Forces and Conservation of Energy

Reducing Unwanted Energy Transfers

1 A man is cycling. The man does work on the pedals to move the bicycle. Some energy is wasted by the bicycle due to friction between the chain and the gears.

State and explain how the man could reduce the amount of energy wasted when cycling.

....

....

[Total 2 marks]

2 A builder is trying to minimise the rate at which a house cools.

a) The builder can build the walls of the house using bricks A-D.
Which type of brick should she use? Tick **one** box.

		Thermal conductivity	Brick thickness (cm)
☐	**A**	High	10
☐	**B**	High	15
☐	**C**	Low	10
☐	**D**	Low	15

[1]

b) The builder uses her electric drill for 1 minute.
Figure 2 shows an incomplete energy transfer diagram for the drill during this time.

Figure 2

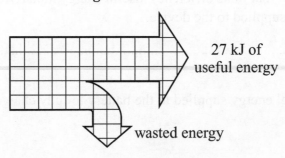

27 kJ of useful energy

wasted energy

Calculate how much energy is supplied to the drill during 1 minute.

Energy supplied = ... kJ
[3]

[Total 4 marks]

Section 17 — Motion, Forces and Conservation of Energy

Energy Resources

Write the energy resources below in the correct column
to show whether they are renewable or non-renewable.

bio-fuel   hydro-electricity

coal

solar

wind   nuclear fuel

tidal

natural gas

oil

Renewable	Non-renewable

1   Petrol or diesel is used to power most cars, like the one in **Figure 1**. They are both made from a fossil fuel.   (Grade 1-3)

Figure 1

a) Name the **three** fossil fuels.

1. ....

2. ....

3. ....

[3]

b) Give **one** other everyday use for fossil fuels.

....

[1]

c) Which of the following energy resources can be used to directly power some modern cars?
Tick **one** box.

☐ **A** Nuclear fuel

☐ **B** Geothermal power

☐ **C** Bio-fuel

☐ **D** Hydro-electricity

[1]

[Total 5 marks]

2   Describe the difference between renewable and non-renewable energy resources.   (Grade 3-4)

....

....

....

[Total 2 marks]

More Energy Resources

1 Tidal barrages use water to generate electricity. *(Grade 3-4)*

a) Which of the following statements about tidal barrages is true?
Tick **one** box.

☐ **A** They generate the same amount of electricity all the time.

☐ **B** They are usually built on top of hills.

☐ **C** They can disturb the habitats of animals.

☐ **D** They produce pollution when generating electricity.

[1]

b) Hydro-electric power plants also use water to generate electricity.
Give **one** advantage of generating electricity using
hydro-electric power plants instead of tidal barrages.

....

....

[1]

[Total 2 marks]

2 A university wants to reduce their energy bills.
They want to build either a single wind turbine nearby,
or install solar panels on top of their buildings. *(Grade 4-5)*

The average wind speed for the university the previous year is shown in **Figure 1**.
The average number of hours of sunlight per day is also given.

Figure 1

	Average wind speed (m/s)	Average number of hours of daylight
October-March	8.0	9
April-September	4.3	15

The university decides to install both a wind turbine and solar panels.
Use the information in **Figure 1** to suggest why.

....

....

....

....

....

....

....

[Total 4 marks]

☹ ☐ ☺ ☐ ☺ ☐

Trends in Energy Resource Use

1 **Figure 1** shows the energy resources used to generate electricity in a country. Grade 3-4

Figure 1

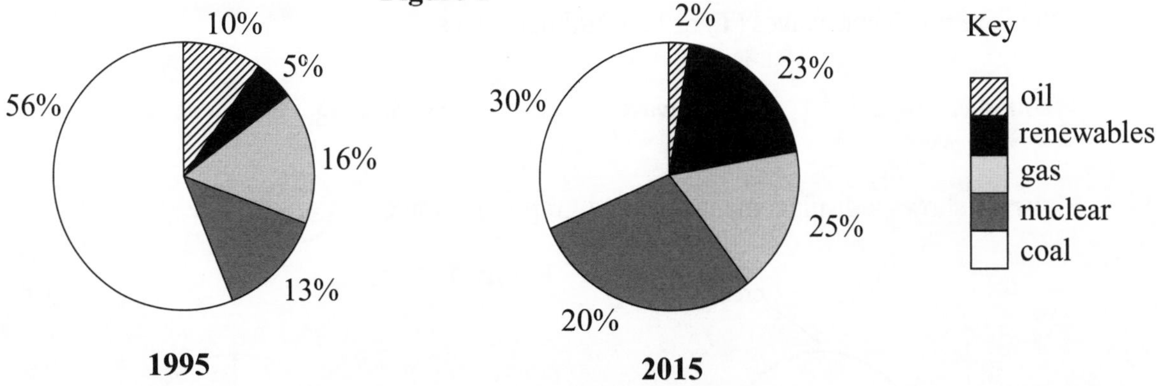
10%
5%
56%
16%
13%
1995
2%
23%
30%
25%
20%
2015
Key
oil
renewables
gas
nuclear
coal

a) Determine what percentage of the country's electricity was generated by fossil fuels in 1995.

.... %
[2]

b) Suggest **one** trend you can determine from the pie charts in **Figure 1**.

....

....
[1]

[Total 3 marks]

2 In the UK, the use of renewable energy resources is increasing. Grade 4-5

a) State and explain **one** possible reason for this increase in the use of renewable energy resources.

....

....

....
[2]

b)* Discuss the factors which may reduce the rate at which we decrease our use of fossil fuels and increase our use of renewable energy resources.

....

....

....

....

....

....

....
[6]

[Total 8 marks]

Wave Basics

1   **Figure 1** shows a displacement-distance graph of a wave.

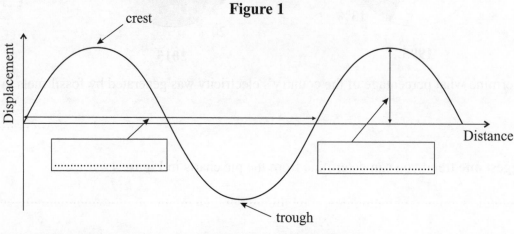

Figure 1

a)   Use phrases from the box to complete the labels in **Figure 1**.

wavelength	period	rest position	amplitude

[2]

b)   State what is meant by the term 'frequency'.

....

[1]

c)   Describe the difference between longitudinal waves and transverse waves.

....

....

....

[2]

[Total 5 marks]

2   A child throws a stone into a puddle. The stone creates ripples
when it hits the water. These ripples spread across the puddle.

The child thinks that a leaf floating on the water's surface will move to the edge
of the puddle with the ripples. Explain whether or not she is correct.

....

....

....

[Total 1 mark]

Wave Speed

1 A ripple produced at the centre of a pond has a wave speed of 0.19 m/s. The ripple travels 114 cm from the centre to the edge of the pond.

Calculate the time taken for the ripple to reach the edge of the pond.
Use the equation:

$$\text{wave speed} = \text{distance} \div \text{time}$$

Time = ... s

[Total 3 marks]

2 A student investigated the speed of sound in air. The equipment she used is shown in **Figure 1**.

The sound waves detected by each microphone were shown as separate traces on the oscilloscope screen.

Figure 1

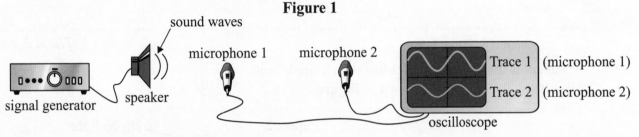

a) Her method is described below in steps **A** to **E**.
Steps **A** to **E** are not in the correct order.

A   Measure the distance between the microphones. This is the wavelength.
B   Stop moving microphone 2 when the traces line up, as shown in **Figure 1**.
C   Use the measured distance and the frequency of the signal generator to find the wave speed.
D   Begin with both microphones at an equal distance from the speaker.
E   Keeping microphone 1 fixed, slowly move microphone 2 away from the speaker. This causes trace 2 to move.

In the spaces below, write down the correct order of steps.
The first one has been done for you.

D → .... → .... → .... → ....

[3]

The signal generator is set to 50.0 Hz. The wavelength of the sound waves is measured to be 6.80 m.

b) State the equation that links wave speed, wavelength and frequency.

....

[1]

c) Calculate the speed of the sound waves.

Wave speed = ... m/s

[2]

[Total 6 marks]

Section 18 — Waves and the Electromagnetic Spectrum

Investigating Waves

1 A student is investigating the waves created in a metal rod. He uses the equipment shown in **Figure 1**.

Grade 3-4

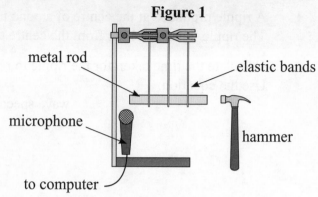

Figure 1

metal rod

elastic bands

microphone

hammer

to computer

The student hits the metal rod with the hammer to create waves in the rod. He knows that the wave with the lowest frequency in the rod has a wavelength of twice the length of the rod. This wave is called the peak frequency wave.

Describe how the student could find the frequency of the peak frequency wave in the rod using the equipment in **Figure 1**.

....

....

....

....

[Total 2 marks]

2* A student is investigating water waves in a ripple tank. She sets up the equipment shown in **Figure 2**.

Grade 4-5

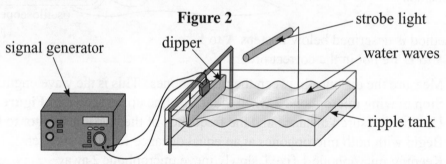

Figure 2

strobe light

dipper

water waves

signal generator

ripple tank

Explain how the student could use this equipment to find the speed of the water waves from the frequency and wavelength of the waves.

....

....

....

....

....

....

....

....

....

....

[Total 6 marks]

Refraction

1 A wave can refract after it hits the boundary between two materials.

Use phrases from the box below to complete the passage about refraction.

| will | changes direction | will not | bounces back | disappears |

Refraction is when a wave .... after it hits a boundary.

A wave that is travelling along the normal ....

refract after it hits the boundary.

[Total 2 marks]

2 A light ray travelling through air hits the boundary of a clear plastic block. The angle of incidence at the air to plastic boundary is 30°. The angle of refraction is 20°.

Complete the ray diagram in **Figure 1** to show the refraction of the light ray at the boundary. The boundary has been drawn for you.

Figure 1

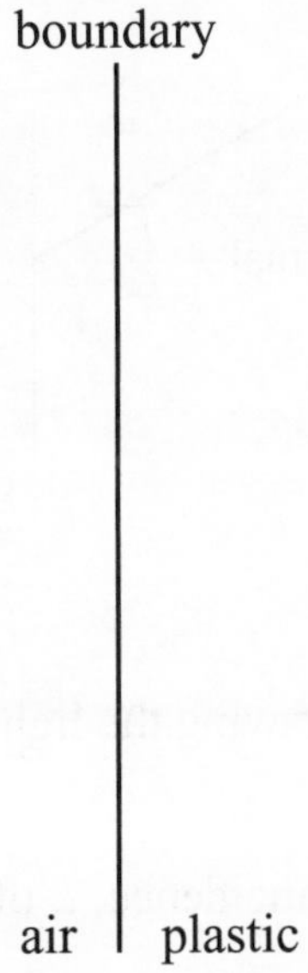

boundary

air | plastic

[Total 4 marks]

3 A ray of light crosses a boundary from air to water. The angle of incidence is 20° and the angle of refraction is 6.5°.

A second ray of light crosses a boundary from water to air. The angle of incidence is 20°. State and explain whether the angle of refraction of this ray will be larger or smaller than 20°.

....

....

....

....

[Total 2 marks]

PRACTICAL   # Investigating Refraction

1   A student is investigating the refraction of light through a glass block.
The student uses a ray box to shine a ray of light into the block.
She traces the path of the ray entering and leaving the block on a sheet
of paper and uses this to measure the angles of incidence and refraction.

a) Explain why a ray box was used for this experiment.

    ....

    ....
                                                                                                        [1]

    Figure 1 is an incomplete diagram showing the path of a ray during the student's investigation.

    Figure 1

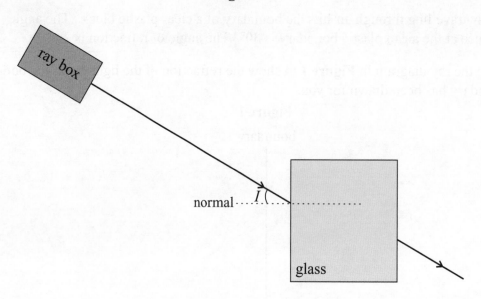

b) Complete the diagram in **Figure 1** by drawing the light ray as it passes through the glass block.
                                                                                                        [1]

c) Using **Figure 1**, determine the angle of incidence, *I*, of the light ray as it enters the glass block.

                                        Angle of incidence = ... °
                                                                                                        [1]

d) The student repeats the experiment for a range of angles of incidence.
    Name **two** things the student should do to make her experiment a fair test.

    1. ....

    2. ....
                                                                                                        [2]
                                                                                            [Total 5 marks]

Exam Practice Tip

If you have to draw rays in the exam, make sure you draw them as neatly and accurately as possible. Use a sharp pencil
so you can draw a clear, thin line and always double check any measurements you've made before you start drawing.

Section 18 — Waves and the Electromagnetic Spectrum

Electromagnetic Waves

1 **Figure 1** shows the electromagnetic spectrum. It is incomplete.

a) Complete **Figure 1** by filling in the missing types of electromagnetic waves.

Figure 1   *[2]*

Radio Waves	....	Infrared	Visible Light	Ultraviolet	....	Gamma Rays

b) Draw an arrow beneath **Figure 1** that points from the electromagnetic waves with the shortest wavelength towards the electromagnetic waves with the longest wavelength.

[1]

c) Use phrases from the box below to complete the following sentences.

a vacuum	glass	sound	longitudinal	transverse	water

All waves in the electromagnetic spectrum are .... waves.

All electromagnetic waves travel at the same speed in ....

[2]

[Total 5 marks]

2 Electromagnetic waves can have a harmful effect on the human body. (Grade 4-5)

a) State how the possible danger of electromagnetic waves is linked to their frequency.

....

[1]

b) Cataracts are an eye condition which may be caused by electromagnetic radiation.
State which type of electromagnetic radiation may cause cataracts.

....

[1]

c) Explain how microwaves can damage the human body.

....

....

[2]

d) Describe the harmful effects on the human body that can be caused by gamma rays.

....

....

[2]

[Total 6 marks]

Exam Practice Tip

You need to know each type of electromagnetic radiation in the EM spectrum for your exam. You also need to be able to put them in order of increasing frequency or wavelength. Remember, visible light is in the middle of the EM spectrum.

Uses of EM Waves

Tick the correct boxes to show if the following
statements about EM waves are **true** or **false**.

	True	False
Radio waves are used to broadcast TV and radio signals.	☐	☐
Radio waves cannot be used to communicate with satellites.	☐	☐
Toasters use infrared radiation to cook food.	☐	☐

1 Microwave radiation can be used to cook food. **Grade 1-3**

a) Use words from the box below to complete the sentences.

emits	reflects	increase	absorbs	decrease

When food is cooked in a microwave oven, water in the food .... microwaves.

This causes the temperature of the food to ....

[2]

b) Give **one** other use of microwave radiation.

....

[1]

[Total 3 marks]

2 A police helicopter, like the one shown in **Figure 1**,
has an infrared camera attached to its base. **Grade 4-5**

Figure 1

a) Which of the following statements about
infrared radiation is correct? Tick **one** box.

☐ **A** The hotter the object, the more infrared radiation it gives out.

☐ **B** The colder the object, the more infrared radiation it gives out.

☐ **C** Hot objects give out no infrared radiation.

☐ **D** All objects give out the same amount of infrared radiation.

[1]

b) Describe how an infrared camera works.

....

....

....

[2]

[Total 3 marks]

Section 18 — Waves and the Electromagnetic Spectrum

More Uses of EM Waves

1 Visible light is the only part of the electromagnetic spectrum our eyes can detect. *(Grade 1-3)*

Which of the following is a use of visible light? Tick **one** box.

- [ ] **A** photography
- [ ] **B** communicating with satellites
- [ ] **C** cooking food
- [ ] **D** disinfecting water

[Total 1 mark]

2 A man marks his wallet with a security pen. The pen contains ink that cannot be seen in visible light. *(Grade 3-4)*

a) Describe how ultraviolet waves can be used to identify the man's wallet if it is stolen.

....

....

[1]

b) Give **one** other security application of ultraviolet waves.

....

[1]

[Total 2 marks]

3 Electromagnetic waves can be used in hospitals. *(Grade 3-4)*

a) Medical tracers that emit gamma rays can be used to detect cancer.
Give **two** other ways gamma rays can be used in hospitals.

1. ....

2. ....

[2]

b) Give **one** other type of electromagnetic radiation which can be used to detect health problems.
Describe how the radiation is used to detect health problems.

Type of EM radiation: ....

Use: ....

[2]

[Total 4 marks]

Exam Practice Tip

Electromagnetic radiation has a lot of uses. Make sure you know at least one use for each part of the EM spectrum. Being able to remember the different uses is an easy way to get yourself some marks in the exam.

The Atomic Model

What is the typical radius of an atom?

☐ 1×10^{-10} m   ☐ 0.01 m   ☐ 0.001 m   ☐ 1×10^{-100} m

1   Relative charge and relative mass are ways of comparing the charges and masses of the particles within an atom.   *(Grade 1-3)*

a)   Use phrases from the box below to complete the passage about atoms.

neutrons	protons	+1	−1	0

.... have a relative charge of +1 and .... have

a relative charge of 0. Electrons have a relative charge of ....

An atom has an overall charge of ....

[4]

b)   State the relative masses for the following particles.

Neutron: ....

Electron: ....

[2]

[Total 6 marks]

2   Atoms are made up of protons, neutrons and electrons.   *(Grade 4-5)*

a)   Describe how protons, neutrons and electrons are arranged in an atom.

....

....

....

[2]

b)   Use your knowledge of relative masses to describe how mass is distributed within the atom.

....

....

....

[2]

[Total 4 marks]

Exam Practice Tip

You need to have an idea of the sizes of atoms and small molecules. Make sure you learn them, they could be an easy way to pick up marks in your exam. And remember, the radius of a nucleus is much smaller than the radius of an atom.

More on the Atomic Model

1 An atom loses an outer electron. (Grade 1-3)

a) What is the name of the particle created when an atom loses an outer electron? Tick **one** box.

☐ **A** Alpha particle   ☐ **C** Ion

☐ **B** Nucleus   ☐ **D** Positron

[1]

b) State the relative charge on this particle.

....

[1]

[Total 2 marks]

2 Electrons orbit the nucleus in different energy levels. (Grade 3-4)

a) State what could cause an electron to move to a higher energy level in an atom.

....

[1]

b) An electron in an atom emits electromagnetic radiation.
Describe how the position of the electron in the atom changes.

....

[1]

[Total 2 marks]

3 Rutherford's alpha particle scattering experiment led to the creation of the first nuclear model of the atom. (Grade 4-5)

a) Name and describe the atomic model that Rutherford's nuclear model replaced.

....

....

[2]

b) State and explain **two** conclusions Rutherford was able to make about the structure of an atom from the results of his alpha particle scattering experiment.

....

....

....

....

....

....

[4]

[Total 6 marks]

 ☐   ☐   ☐

Isotopes and Nuclear Radiation

The standard notation used to represent atoms is shown.
Use the phrases on the right to correctly fill in the labels.

electron number

neutron number

mass number

element symbol

charge   atomic number

$_Z^A X$

1   Some isotopes are unstable. These isotopes emit nuclear radiation.   **Grade 3-4**

a) Draw **one** line from each term on the left to its correct definition on the right.

Term

| Gamma rays |

| Isotopes |

| Alpha particles |

Definition

| Atoms whose nuclei have the same positive charge but different nuclear masses. |

| Particles that are the same as helium nuclei. |

| Electromagnetic radiation from the nucleus. |

[2]

b) An unstable isotope decays. It releases a high-speed electron from its nucleus.
Name this type of radioactive decay.

....

[1]

[Total 3 marks]

2   Beta-minus sources are used when making paper. The sources
are used to check the thickness of the paper. The source is placed
on one side of the paper and a detector is placed on the other side.
Some of the beta-minus particles pass through the paper. The amount of
radiation that passes through the paper is measured. The paper is then
made thicker or thinner depending on the amount of radiation measured.   **Grade 4-5**

Explain why a source that emits alpha particles or gamma rays couldn't be used for this purpose.

....

....

....

....

[Total 2 marks]

Nuclear Equations

1   A strontium-90 nucleus decays to form yttrium-90.
The nuclear equation for this decay is shown to the right.   **Grade 3-4** $${}^{90}_{38}\text{Sr} \rightarrow {}^{90}_{39}\text{Y} + {}^{0}_{-1}\beta$$

a) Describe how the mass and atomic numbers of the nucleus change during the decay.

Mass number: ....

Atomic number: ....

[2]

b) Explain how the charge of the nucleus changes during this decay.

....

....

[2]

[Total 4 marks]

2   A carbon nucleus decays into a boron nucleus by beta-plus decay.
Describe the changes that occur in the nucleus during the beta-plus decay.   **Grade 3-4**

....

....

[Total 2 marks]

3   Nuclear equations are a way of showing radioactive decay.   **Grade 4-5**

The following nuclear equation shows a nitrogen nucleus undergoing radioactive decay.

$$^{24}_{7}\text{N} \rightarrow {}^{a}_{b}\text{N} + {}^{1}_{0}\text{X}$$

a) i) Name the particle represented by **X** in the nuclear equation above.

....

[1]

ii) Calculate the values of *a* and *b*.

a = ...

b = ...

[2]

b) A polonium (Po) nucleus has an atomic number of 84 and a mass number of 218.
It decays by alpha decay to a lead (Pb) nucleus.
Write a balanced nuclear equation to show this decay.

....

[3]

[Total 6 marks]

Background Radiation and Activity

1 A teacher determines the activity of a radioactive source. **Grade 1-3**

a) What unit is activity measured in? Tick **one** box.

☐ **A** Seconds

☐ **B** Sieverts

☐ **C** Becquerels

☐ **D** Decays

[1]

b) Describe how the activity of a radioactive source changes over time.

....

[1]

[Total 2 marks]

2 A student wants to investigate the radioactivity of a radioactive source. Her teacher says that she must take background radiation into account whenever she takes measurements. **Grade 3-4**

a) State what is meant by 'background radiation'.

....

[1]

b) Name **two** sources of background radiation.

1. ....

2. ....

[2]

c) The student uses a Geiger-Müller tube and counter to detect radiation from the source. Describe the steps the student should take to make sure her method takes into account background radiation.

....

....

....

[2]

d) Name **one** other piece of equipment the student could use to detect radiation from the source.

....

[1]

[Total 6 marks]

Exam Practice Tip

Activity is a really important thing to get your head around. Remember it's the rate of decay of a radioactive source.

Half-Life

1 Half-life can be used to describe how the activity of a sample changes over time. *Grade 1-3*

a) State what is meant by 'half-life'. Your answer should refer to the activity of the sample.

....

....
[1]

b) Use phrases from the box below to complete the passage about radioactive decay.

predictable	can	random	can't	large	small

Radioactive decay is a .... process. This means you ....

predict when a certain nucleus will decay. If you have a ....

number of nuclei in a sample, you can use the half-life to predict the activity of the sample.
[3]

[Total 4 marks]

2 **Figure 1** shows how the activity of a radioactive sample changes over time. *Grade 4-5*

Figure 1

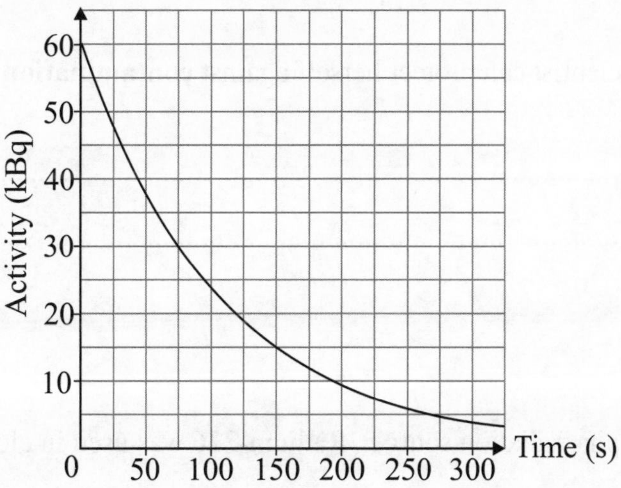

a) Use **Figure 1** to determine the half-life of the sample.

Half-life = ... s
[1]

b) The sample initially contained 6 500 000 undecayed nuclei.
Predict how many of these nuclei will remain after the first 150 seconds.
Give your answer to 2 significant figures.

Number of remaining nuclei = ...
[3]

[Total 4 marks]

Section 19 — Radioactivity

Irradiation and Contamination

1   Workers in a nuclear power station are at risk of being irradiated by nuclear radiation. **Grade 1-3**
    Which of the following methods would reduce their risk of irradiation? Tick **one** box.

☐   **A** Work behind barriers that absorb radiation.

☐   **B** Keep fire extinguishers close by.

☐   **C** Wear photographic film badges.

☐   **D** Wash hands regularly.

[Total 1 mark]

2   A scientist is looking at how to reduce her risk of contamination **Grade 4-5**
    and irradiation while working with radioactive sources.

a) State what is meant by 'contamination' and 'irradiation'.

....

....

....

....

[2]

b) Give **two** ways the scientist can protect herself against **contamination** when handling
    radioactive sources.

1. ....

2. ....

[2]

[Total 4 marks]

3   Radium-226 is an alpha radiation source. Radium-226 was used in clocks until the 1960s. **Grade 4-5**

State whether a clockmaker should be more worried about contamination or irradiation
when working on clocks made before 1960. Explain your answer.

....

....

....

....

....

....

[Total 3 marks]

Section 19 — Radioactivity

Energy Transfers and Systems

Warm-Up

Draw a circle around all the types of energy store on the right.

sound   volcanic   thermal

elastic potential   nuclear   radioactive

---

1   An apple is falling from a tree. **Figure 1** shows an incomplete diagram of the energy transfer that occurs. Use words from the box below to complete the diagram.

| kinetic | chemical | electrostatic | gravitational potential | magnetic |

Figure 1

....   mechanically   ....
energy store of the apple   →   energy store of the apple

[Total 2 marks]

---

2   Whenever a system changes, energy is transferred.

a) Some energy is always dissipated when a system changes.
State what is meant by 'dissipated'.

....

....

[1]

b) Complete the table below to show whether each statement about closed systems is true or false.
Tick **one** box in each row.

Statement	True	False
Energy can be transferred between stores in a closed system.		
There can be no net change in the total energy of a closed system.		
Energy can be transferred into and out of a closed system.		

[3]

[Total 4 marks]

Exam Practice Tip

Make sure you know the different types of energy store. Remember that energy can be transferred between stores mechanically (because of a force doing work), electrically, by heating or by radiation (e.g. light and sound waves).

Forces and Work Done

1 The Earth and the Moon interact at a distance without contact. There is a force of attraction acting between them.

Which row of the table correctly describes the force acting between the Earth and the Moon? Tick **one** box.

	Force acting	Cause of force
☐ **A**	gravitational	interacting gravitational fields
☐ **B**	electrostatic	interacting gravitational fields
☐ **C**	gravitational	interacting electric fields
☐ **D**	electrostatic	interacting electric fields

[Total 1 mark]

2 **Figure 1** shows an ice hockey puck on ice. The puck is moving towards the right. It has two contact forces acting on it.

Complete the diagram by labelling the two forces.

Figure 1

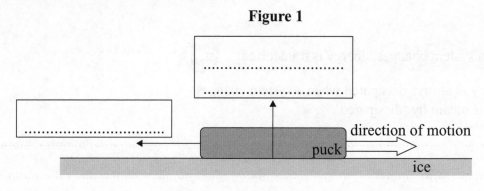

[Total 2 marks]

3 A man pushes a trolley along a supermarket aisle for 15 m. He applies a horizontal force of 50 N.

a) Calculate the work done by the man. Use the equation:

work done = force × distance moved in the direction of the force

Work done = ... Nm

[2]

b) State the amount of energy transferred to the trolley.

Energy transferred = ... J

[1]

[Total 3 marks]

Wasted Energy and Power

1 A person is riding a bike. Energy is transferred mechanically to the kinetic energy store of the bike chain. The bike chain heats up as the person is cycling. *(Grade 3-4)*

a) Explain how you know this process is wasteful.

....

....

....

[2]

b) Suggest a way to reduce how wasteful this process is.

....

[1]

[Total 3 marks]

2 A student heats a beaker of water using an immersion heater. The immersion heater has a power of 35 W. *(Grade 4-5)*

a) Calculate the work done by the immersion heater when it is used for 600 s.
Use the equation:

$$\text{power} = \frac{\text{work done}}{\text{time taken}}$$

Work done = ... J

[3]

b) The student then uses the immersion heater to heat a second beaker of water.
The heater transfers 16 800 J of energy. Calculate the time that the heater was on for.

Time = ... s

[3]

[Total 6 marks]

3 1200 kJ of energy is transferred to a kettle. The kettle has an efficiency of 0.7. Calculate how much energy is transferred usefully to the thermal energy store of the water inside. Give your answer in joules. *(Grade 4-5)*

Energy transferred usefully = ... J

[Total 3 marks]

Current and Circuits

Warm-Up

Draw lines to match each circuit symbol to its correct name.

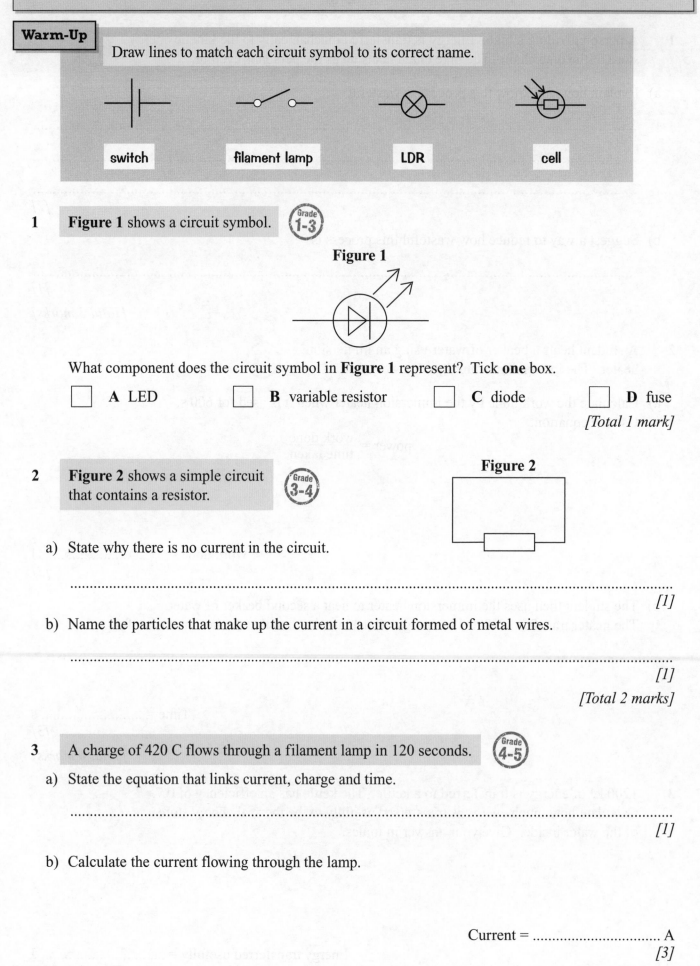

switch   filament lamp   LDR   cell

1   **Figure 1** shows a circuit symbol. Grade 1-3

Figure 1

What component does the circuit symbol in **Figure 1** represent? Tick **one** box.

☐ **A** LED   ☐ **B** variable resistor   ☐ **C** diode   ☐ **D** fuse

[Total 1 mark]

2   **Figure 2** shows a simple circuit that contains a resistor. Grade 3-4

Figure 2

a) State why there is no current in the circuit.

....

[1]

b) Name the particles that make up the current in a circuit formed of metal wires.

....

[1]

[Total 2 marks]

3   A charge of 420 C flows through a filament lamp in 120 seconds. Grade 4-5

a) State the equation that links current, charge and time.

....

[1]

b) Calculate the current flowing through the lamp.

Current = ... A

[3]

[Total 4 marks]

Potential Difference and Resistance

For each statement, circle whether it is **true** or **false**.

Potential difference is the energy transferred per coulomb of charge passed.	True / False
One volt is one ampere per coulomb.	True / False
Electrical current does work against electrical resistance.	True / False

1 A filament lamp has a potential difference across it of 18 V.

a) Which equation relates energy transferred, charge moved and potential difference?
Tick **one** box.

☐ **A** $E = Q \times V$

☐ **B** $E = Q \div V$

☐ **C** $E = Q - V$

☐ **D** $E = \frac{1}{2}(Q \times V)$

[1]

b) 150 C of charge moves through the lamp wire.
Calculate the energy transferred to the filament lamp.

Energy transferred = ... J

[2]

[Total 3 marks]

2 A potential difference of 25 V is applied across a resistor. A current of
3.0 A flows through the resistor, causing it to increase in temperature.

a) Give the equation that links potential difference, current and resistance.

....

[1]

b) Calculate the resistance of the resistor. Give your answer to 2 significant figures.

Resistance = ... Ω

[3]

c) Explain why the current through the resistor decreases as the resistor gets hotter.

....

....

....

[2]

[Total 6 marks]

I-V Graphs

1 I-V graphs can be used to find the resistances of electrical components.

a) Which of the graphs in **Figure 1** below is the correct *I-V* graph of a diode? Tick **one** box.

Figure 1

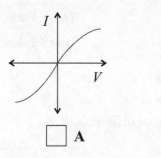 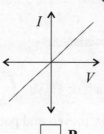 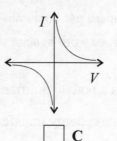 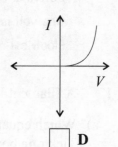

☐ **A**   ☐ **B**   ☐ **C**   ☐ **D**

[1]

b) Describe what the *I-V* graph shows about the resistance of a diode.

....

....

[2]

[Total 3 marks]

PRACTICAL

2 A student is investigating how current changes with potential difference for a filament lamp. She uses the circuit shown in **Figure 2**.

Figure 2

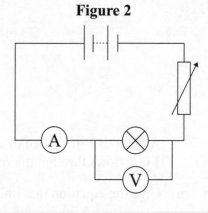

a) Describe a method the student could use to investigate how current changes with potential difference for the filament lamp.

....

....

....

....

....

....

[3]

b) **Figure 3** shows the *I-V* graph plotted from her results.

Using **Figure 3**, calculate the resistance of the filament lamp when the current through it is 2.0 A.

Figure 3

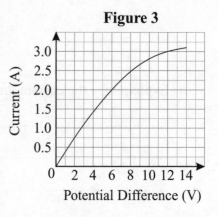

Resistance = ... Ω

[4]

[Total 7 marks]

Section 21 — Electricity and Circuits

Circuit Devices

1   A thermistor is a type of resistor.

Which of the graphs below shows how the resistance of a thermistor changes with temperature?
Tick **one** box.

Figure 1

☐   **A**

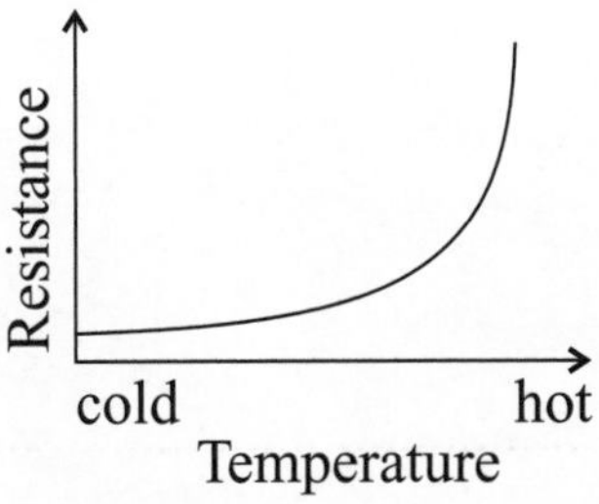

☐   **C**

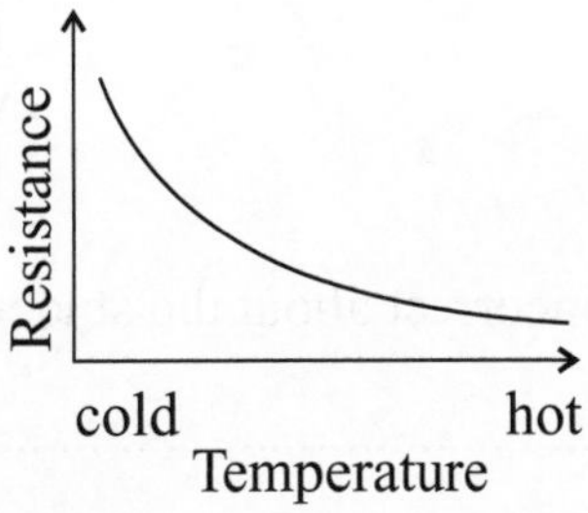

☐   **B**

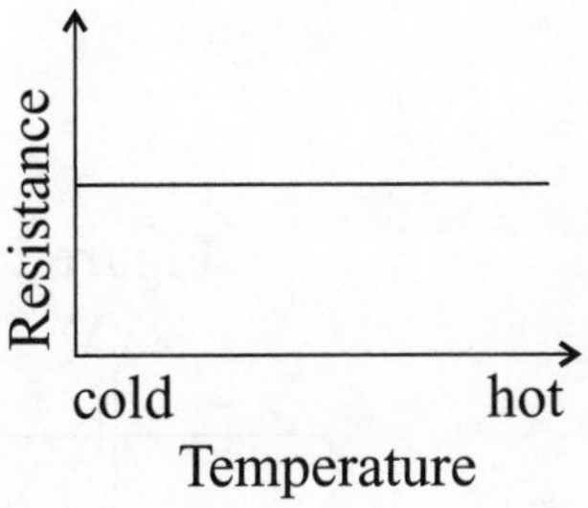

☐   **D**

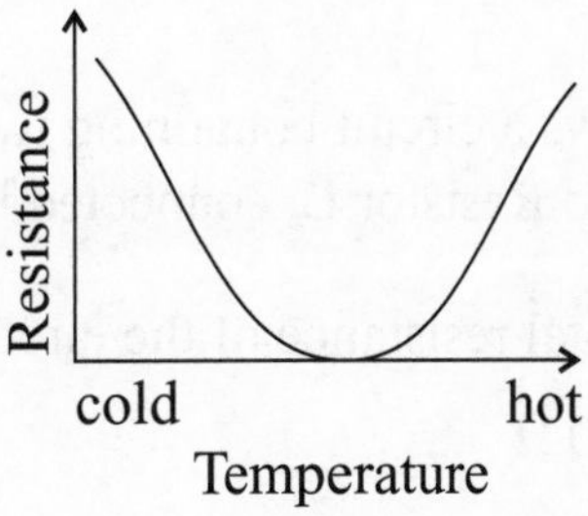

[Total 1 mark]

2   A student wants to measure the resistance of a light dependent resistor (LDR).

a)   Draw the circuit diagram of a circuit that the student could use to measure
the resistance of an LDR. Use the circuit symbols shown in **Figure 2**.

Figure 2

battery	voltmeter	ammeter	LDR
	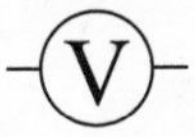		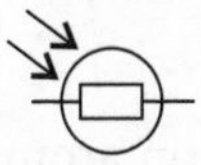

[2]

b)   The resistance of an LDR depends on its surroundings.
State what happens to the resistance of an LDR as the surrounding light intensity increases.

....

[1]

[Total 3 marks]

Section 21 — Electricity and Circuits

Series and Parallel Circuits

1 A student wants to measure the potential difference across a filament bulb that is in series with a resistor. She sets up a circuit as shown in the diagram in **Figure 1**.

Figure 1

State what is incorrect about the student's circuit.

....

[Total 1 mark]

2 **Figure 2** shows a circuit containing two resistors, Resistor A and Resistor B, connected in series.

a) What is the total resistance of the circuit? Tick **one** box.

☐ **A** 10 Ω
☐ **B** 30 Ω
☐ **C** 20 Ω
☐ **D** 60 Ω

[1]

Figure 2

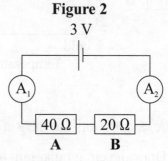

b) State and explain which resistor has the higher potential difference across it.

....

....

[1]

c) The reading on ammeter A₁ in **Figure 2** is 0.05 A.
Write down the reading on ammeter A₂.

Current = ... A

[1]

d) Resistor A has a potential difference across it of 2 V.
Resistor A is moved so it is connected in parallel to Resistor B.
Calculate the change in potential difference across Resistor B.

Change in potential difference = ... V

[3]

[Total 6 marks]

Exam Practice Tip

Make sure you know the differences between potential difference, current and resistance for series and parallel circuits.
In all circuit diagrams, make sure that the wires are straight lines and the circuit is closed (otherwise it won't work).

More on Series and Parallel Circuits

1 A series circuit containing a resistor and a battery is set up. A second, identical resistor is added to the circuit. The two resistors are in parallel.

Grade 4-5

State and explain how the resistance of the circuit changes when the second resistor is added.

....

....

....

....

....

....

[Total 4 marks]

PRACTICAL

2* A student sets up the basic circuit shown in **Figure 1**.
Describe an experiment the student could do using this circuit to investigate how adding identical fixed resistors in parallel affects the overall resistance of a circuit. You may wish to add to the circuit diagram in **Figure 1** as part of your answer.

Grade 4-5

Figure 1

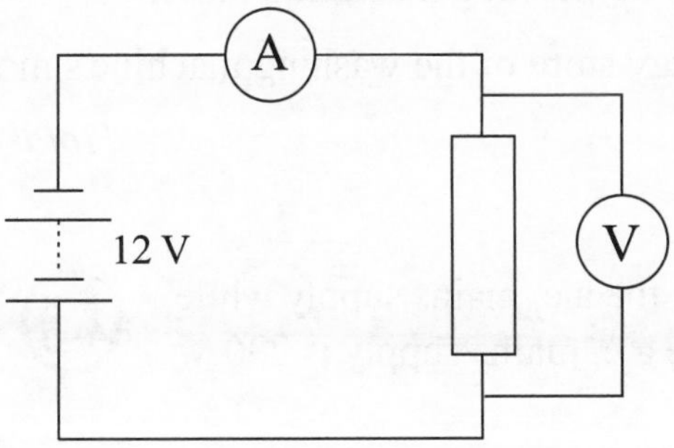

12 V

....

....

....

....

....

....

....

....

[Total 6 marks]

Energy in Circuits

Use the phrases below to complete the sentences about energy transfers.

| surroundings | by heating | kinetic | thermal | electrically |

To toast a slice of bread a toaster transfers energy.

Energy is transferred from the a.c mains supply to the thermal energy stores

of the toaster's heating coils ....

Energy is then transferred .... to the ....

energy stores of the bread and the ....

---

1 The power source for a washing machine is the a.c. mains supply. **(Grade 1-3)**

Which of the following is the main energy transfer from
the a.c. mains supply to the washing machine? Tick **one** box.

- [ ] **A** By heating to the electrostatic energy store of the washing machine's motor.
- [ ] **B** Electrically to the nuclear energy store of the washing machine's motor.
- [ ] **C** Electrically to the kinetic energy store of the washing machine's motor.
- [ ] **D** Mechanically to the elastic potential energy store of the washing machine's motor.

[Total 1 mark]

---

2 An electric hob transfers 48 300 J in 30 seconds from the a.c. mains supply while **(Grade 4-5)**
heating a pan of soup. The potential difference of the a.c. mains supply is 230 V.

a) Calculate the current through the hob.
Use an equation from the Equations List.

Current = ... A

[3]

b) The hob works due to the heating effect of an electric current. Describe **one** situation
other than cooking where the heating effect of an electric current can be useful.

....

....

[1]

[Total 4 marks]

Electrical Power

1   **Figure 1** shows a circuit. The reading on the voltmeter is 6 V.

Figure 1

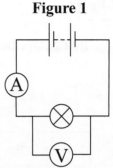

a) The reading on the ammeter in **Figure 1** is 2 A.
    Calculate the electrical power of the filament lamp. Use the equation:

$$\text{electrical power} = \text{current} \times \text{potential difference}$$

Electrical power = ... W

[2]

b) State the equation that links power, energy transferred and time taken.

....

[1]

c) Calculate the energy transferred to the lamp when it is on for 30 seconds.

Energy transferred = ... J

[3]

[Total 6 marks]

2   A lawnmower motor circuit has a power rating of 1250 W and a resistance of 8.0 Ω.

Calculate the current flowing through the lawnmower motor. Use the equation:

$$\text{electrical power} = \text{current squared} \times \text{resistance}$$

Current = ... A

[Total 3 marks]

Exam Practice Tip

There's a lot of equations to do with power, but try not to panic about them. If you're not sure which one to use, look at the values you've been given, or have already calculated in the question. Then use the equation which uses those.

Electricity in the Home

In the table below, put a tick next to each statement to show whether it applies to direct current or alternating current.

	Direct current	Alternating current
The type of current supplied by a battery		
The type of current where the direction of movement of the charge is in one direction		
The type of current supplied by the UK domestic supply		
The type of current where the direction of movement of the charge changes direction		

1 Most houses in the UK are connected to the domestic electricity supply. Grade 3-4

a) State the voltage and frequency of the UK domestic electricity supply.

Voltage = ...V

Frequency = ... Hz

[2]

b) A kettle is plugged into the domestic supply with a cable containing a live wire, a neutral wire and an earth wire.

i) The live wire carries an alternating voltage.
Describe the difference between a direct voltage and an alternating voltage.

....

....

....

[2]

ii) Complete the table in **Figure 1** to show the sizes of the potential differences between the wires that make up a typical electrical cable.

Figure 1

Wires	Potential difference / V
Live wire and neutral wire	....
Neutral wire and earth wire	....
Earth wire and live wire	....

[3]

[Total 7 marks]

Section 21 — Electricity and Circuits

Electrical Safety

1 Most electric cables used for domestic appliances have a live, neutral and earth wire.
State which wire would be dangerous to touch in an electric cable if the wire was exposed.

Grade 1-3

....

[Total 1 mark]

2 **Figure 1** shows an electric cable connecting an iron to the domestic electricity supply
that has become worn with use. There is no insulation covering part of the live wire.

Grade 3-4

Figure 1

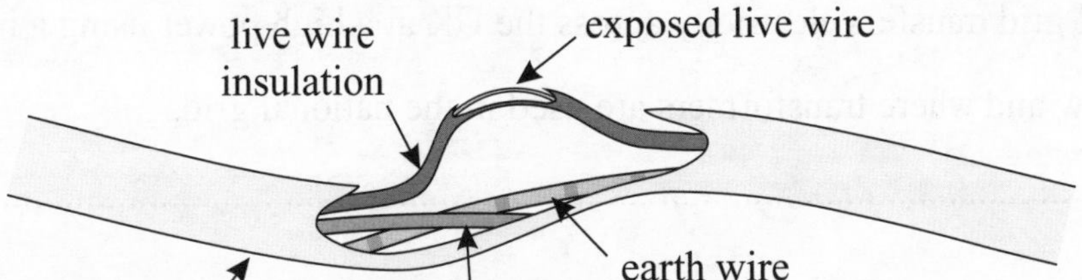

live wire insulation   exposed live wire

cable insulation   neutral wire insulation   earth wire insulation

State and explain what would happen if a person touched the exposed live wire.

....

....

....

[Total 3 marks]

3 Many electrical devices with metal casing include an earth wire and fuse.

Grade 4-5

a) If a live wire comes loose and touches the metal casing a large current will flow through the live
wire, the fuse and the earth wire. Describe how the fuse protects the device in this situation.

....

....

....

[2]

b) State why fuses should be used in the electrical circuits of a house.

....

[1]

c) Name another component that can be used in place of a household fuse.

....

[1]

[Total 4 marks]

Transformers and the National Grid

1 Which of the following correctly describes the effect of a step-down transformer? Tick **one** box.

(Grade 3-4)

☐ **A** It increases the output current and the output potential difference.

☐ **B** It increases the output current and decreases the output potential difference.

☐ **C** It decreases the output current and increases the output potential difference.

☐ **D** It decreases the output current and the output potential difference.

[Total 1 mark]

2 The national grid transfers electricity across the UK at a high power using a high voltage.

(Grade 4-5)

a) Describe how and where transformers are used in the national grid.

....

....

[2]

b) Explain why the national grid is an efficient way of transferring energy.

....

....

....

....

[3]

[Total 5 marks]

3 A transformer is 100% efficient. The transformer steps up a 20 V supply to 240 V. The current in the secondary coil is 0.5 A. Calculate the current through the primary coil. Use an equation from the Equations List.

(Grade 4-5)

Current = ... A

[Total 3 marks]

Exam Practice Tip

Make sure you're careful when rearranging the equation for transformers. It can look big and scary, but don't panic. Just remember that whatever you do to one side of the equation, you must do to the other side of the equation.

Magnets and Magnetic Fields

Two pairs of magnets are shown. Forces act between each pair of magnets. Circle the correct word to show whether the forces between the magnets are attractive or repulsive.

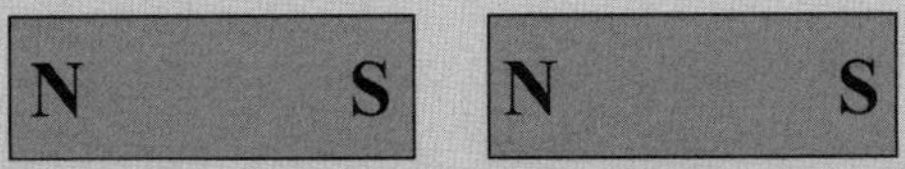

N   S   N   S   N   S   S   N

attractive / repulsive   attractive / repulsive

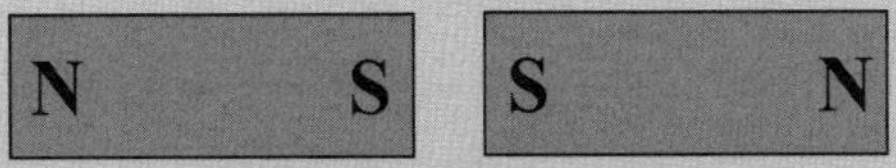

1   Two bar magnets are placed near to each other, as shown in **Figure 1**.   *Grade 1-3*
     Sketch the uniform magnetic field between the two poles.

Figure 1

N   S

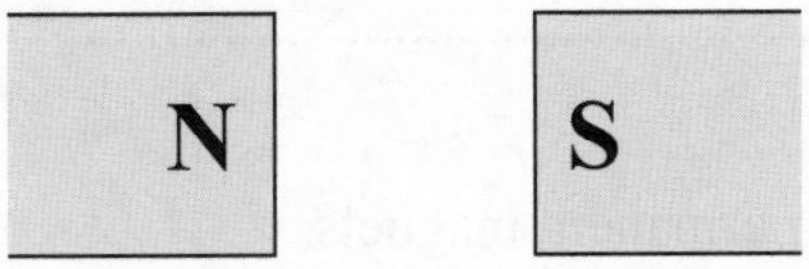

[Total 2 marks]

2   **Figure 2** shows a bar magnet.   *Grade 3-4*

Figure 2

N   S

a)   Sketch the magnetic field lines around the bar magnet in **Figure 2**.

[2]

b)   Another bar magnet has a stronger magnetic field than the magnet in **Figure 2**.
     Describe how the field lines around this magnet would be different from the ones drawn in part a).

....

[1]

[Total 3 marks]

Exam Practice Tip

Make sure you use a sharp pencil for any drawings in the exam. When drawing magnetic field lines, draw enough lines so you can clearly see the overall shape of the field, and don't forget to add arrows to show the direction of the field.

Permanent and Induced Magnets

1 Steel is a temporary magnetic material.
Name **two** other temporary magnetic materials.

Grade 1-3

1. ....

2. ....

[Total 2 marks]

2 Magnets can be permanent or induced.

Grade 3-4

a) Describe the difference between permanent and induced magnets.

....

....

....

[2]

b) Describe **one** everyday use of permanent magnets.

....

....

[1]

[Total 3 marks]

3 A block of cobalt is held in place near to a permanent magnet, as shown in **Figure 1**.

Grade 4-5

Figure 1

N	**S**		•P
permanent magnet		cobalt	

a) A steel paperclip is placed against the block of cobalt at point P, shown in **Figure 1**.
The paperclip sticks to the block of cobalt.
State what has happened to the block of cobalt to cause the paperclip to stick to it.

....

[1]

b) The bar magnet is removed. Explain what happens to the paperclip.

....

....

....

[2]

[Total 3 marks]

Electromagnetism and Solenoids

1   A long piece of wire can be wound into a solenoid.

a) Use phrases from the box below to complete the passage about solenoids.

a permanent magnet	add together	cancel out
an electromagnet	weaker	stronger

A solenoid with a current flowing through it is an example of ....

Outside of the solenoid, the field lines of each coil ....

to create a .... magnetic field than inside the solenoid.

[3]

b) Name **one** piece of equipment that could be used to show the shape and direction of the magnetic field produced around a solenoid.

....

[1]

[Total 4 marks]

2   **Figure 1** shows a wire with a current flowing through it. The direction of the current is out of the page. Grade 4-5

Figure 1

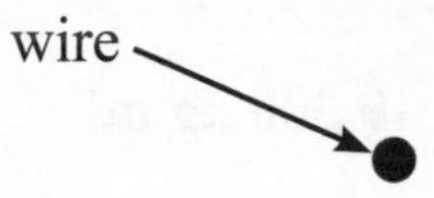

wire ●

Figure 2

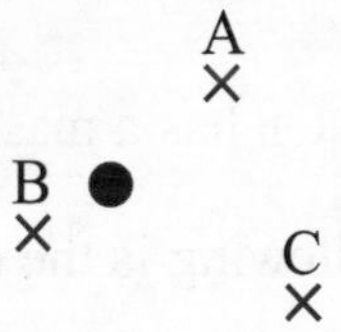

A
×
B ●
×   C
×

a) Complete **Figure 1** by drawing the magnetic field produced by the current in the wire.

[2]

b) **Figure 2** shows three points around the same wire. State at which point, **A**, **B** or **C**, the magnetic field is strongest.

....

[1]

c) The current through the wire is increased. The direction of the current is also reversed. Describe how this affects the magnetic field produced by the current in the wire.

....

....

....

[2]

[Total 5 marks]

Density

1 An irregularly-shaped stone has an unknown volume. *(Grade 1-3)*

What equipment can be used for finding the volume of the stone? Tick **one** box.

☐ **A** a thermometer ☐ **B** a displacement can ☐ **C** a balance ☐ **D** a ruler

[Total 1 mark]

PRACTICAL

2 A student has a balance, a measuring cylinder and some acid (a liquid). *(Grade 4-5)*
She wants to use the equipment to find the density of the acid.

Describe an experiment the student could do to calculate the density of the acid.

....

....

....

....

....

....

....

[Total 4 marks]

3 A block of tungsten has a mass of 7720 kg. Tungsten has a density of 19 300 kg/m^3. *(Grade 4-5)*

a) Which of the following is the correct equation for volume? Tick **one** box.

☐ **A** volume = density × mass

☐ **B** volume = density ÷ mass

☐ **C** volume = mass ÷ density

☐ **D** volume = ½ × density × mass

[1]

b) Calculate the volume of the block of tungsten.

Volume = ... m^3
[2]

c) A 0.12 m^3 sample is cut from the block. Calculate the mass of the sample.
Give your answer to 2 significant figures.

Mass = ... kg
[3]

[Total 6 marks]

Kinetic Theory and States of Matter

Warm-Up

The images below show the particles in a substance when it is in three different states of matter. Label each image to show whether the substance is a solid, a liquid or a gas.

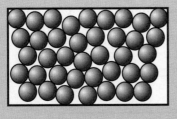 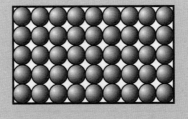 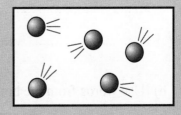

....

1 Heating or cooling a substance can lead to a change of state. (Grade 1-3)

a) Describe the following changes of state:

Melting: ....

Freezing: ....

Condensing: ....

[3]

b) A change of state is a physical change.
Use phrases from the box below to complete the passage.

will	also called	will not	different to

A physical change is .... a chemical change. If you reverse a

physical change, the substance .... get back its original properties.

[2]

[Total 5 marks]

2 A student fills a test tube with 30 g of water. He then heats the water so that it boils. (Grade 4-5)
The student's experiment is set up so that any water vapour produced is collected.

After a short time, the student stops boiling the water.
The mass of the water in the test tube is now 20 g.
State the mass of the water vapour collected by the student. Explain your answer.

....

....

....

....

....

[Total 2 marks]

Specific Heat Capacity

1 Different substances have different specific heat capacities. (Grade 1-3)

a) State what is meant by the 'specific heat capacity' of a substance.

....

....

[1]

b) Use words from the box below to complete the passage.

electrical	reduce	thermal	increase

Materials with high specific heat capacities are good .... insulators.

They can be used to .... energy transfers by heating.

[2]

[Total 3 marks]

2 A block of aluminium is heated. The total amount of energy transferred to the block is 9000 J. The mass of the block is 200 g. (Grade 4-5)

a) The temperature of the block increases by 50 °C.
Calculate the specific heat capacity of aluminium.
Use an equation from the Equations List.

Specific heat capacity = ... J/kg°C

[3]

b) Describe what happened to the particles in the aluminium as it was heated.
Explain how this resulted in a change in the temperature of the aluminium.

....

....

....

....

....

....

[3]

[Total 6 marks]

Specific Latent Heat

Warm-Up

Which of the following is the correct definition of specific latent heat? Tick **one** box.

The energy needed to raise the temperature of a substance by 1 °C. ☐

The maximum amount of energy an object can store before it melts. ☐

The energy needed to change the state of 1 kg of a substance without changing its temperature. ☐

The energy needed to change the state of 10 kg of a substance without changing its temperature. ☐

---

1 Explain the difference between specific heat capacity and specific latent heat. **Grade 3-4**

....

....

....

[Total 2 marks]

---

2 A student melts a sample of ice. **Grade 4-5**

a) 183.7 kJ of energy is transferred to the ice to completely melt it.
The temperature of the ice does not change during this time.
The specific latent heat of fusion for ice is 334 000 J/kg.
Calculate the mass of the sample. Use an equation from the Equations List.

Mass = ... kg
[3]

b) The ice is then heated until all of the sample boils and becomes a gas.
The specific latent heat of vaporisation of water is 2 260 000 J/kg.

Calculate the energy needed to completely boil the sample without changing its temperature.
Give your answer to 2 significant figures.

Energy = ... J
[3]

[Total 6 marks]

Exam Practice Tip

Watch out for units whenever you're doing calculations. The energies involved in changes of state are usually pretty large, so you may be given information in kJ instead of J. If you get an answer that seems too big or too small, check through your working to see if you've missed a unit conversion — it's an easy way to lose marks in the exam.

 ☐   ☐   ☐

Section 23 — Matter

Investigating Water

1 **Figure 1** shows a temperature-time graph for a sample of ice as it is heated.

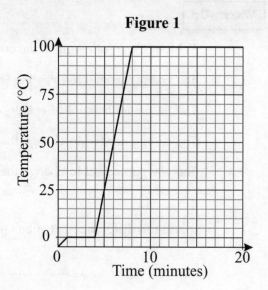
Figure 1

a) State what is happening to the ice 2 minutes after heating began.

....

[1]

b) Determine how long the sample was heated for before it began to boil.

....

[1]

[Total 2 marks]

2 A student is investigating the specific heat capacity of water. The setup of her equipment is shown in **Figure 2**.

Figure 2

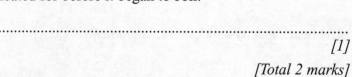

Using her setup, the student supplied 60 g of water with 3050 J of energy. The student repeated her experiment five times. **Figure 3** shows her results.

a) Calculate the average temperature change for the water.

Figure 3

	Trial 1	Trial 2	Trial 3	Trial 4	Trial 5	Average
Temperature Change (°C)	11.9	12.2	9.1	11.9	12.0	....

[2]

b) Calculate the specific heat capacity of water.
Use the average temperature change calculated in part a).
Give your answer to 2 significant figures. Use the equation:

$$\text{specific heat capacity} = \frac{\text{change in thermal energy}}{\text{mass} \times \text{change in temperature}}$$

Specific heat capacity = ... J/kg°C

[3]

[Total 5 marks]

Particle Motion in Gases

Which of the following temperatures is equal to absolute zero? Tick **one** box.

| | -273 °C | | 0 °C | | 237 °C | | 273 °C |

1 Describe, in terms of the movement of particles, what is meant by the term 'absolute zero'. *(Grade 3-4)*

....

....

[Total 1 mark]

2 An oven is at a temperature of 155 °C. Calculate this temperature in kelvin. *(Grade 3-4)*

Temperature = ... K

[Total 1 mark]

3 A fixed amount of gas is in a sealed container. *(Grade 4-5)*

a) Describe how pressure is created by the gas particles in the container.

....

....

....

....

....

[3]

b) The sealed container and the gas are then heated. The volume of the container does not change. Explain how the pressure of the gas inside the container changes.

....

....

....

....

....

[3]

[Total 6 marks]

Forces and Elasticity

1 **Figure 1** shows a force-extension graph for an elastic object. (Grade 1-3)

Which of the following options describes the relationship between force and extension at point X? Tick **one** box.

☐ **A** squared

☐ **B** non-linear

☐ **C** linear

☐ **D** inverse

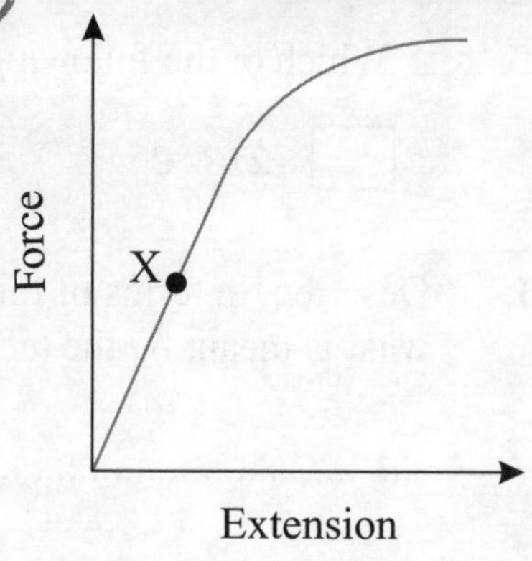

[Total 1 mark]

Figure 1

[Graph showing Force on vertical axis, Extension on horizontal axis, with a curve that rises and levels off. Point X is marked on the lower part of the curve.]

2 A spring is stretched elastically by 0.08 m. The spring constant of the spring is 250 N/m. (Grade 3-4)

Calculate the force exerted on the spring.
Use the equation:

force exerted on a spring = spring constant × extension

Force exerted = ... N

[Total 2 marks]

3 A student pulls on either end of a spring. This causes the spring to stretch. (Grade 3-4)

a) Two forces are being applied to the spring to make it stretch.
Explain why more than one force is needed to make the spring stretch.

....

....

[1]

b) The student pulls the spring so hard that it stops distorting elastically and begins to distort inelastically. Describe the difference between elastic and inelastic distortion.

....

....

....

[2]

[Total 3 marks]

Exam Practice Tip

Don't panic if you see a spring question that talks about compression instead of extension — you can still use the equation from question 2. Remember though, you can only use the equation for distortions that are <u>linear</u>.

 ☐ ☐ ☐

Investigating Elasticity

PRACTICAL

1   A student is investigating the relationship between the extension of a spring and the force acting on it. He hangs unit masses from the bottom of a spring to stretch it. He measures the extension of the spring for each force applied to the spring.

Figure 1 shows the student's results.
Figure 2 is an incomplete force-extension graph of the results.

Figure 1

Force (N)	Extension (cm)
0.0	0.0
1.0	4.0
2.0	8.0
3.0	12.0
4.0	16.0
5.0	20.0

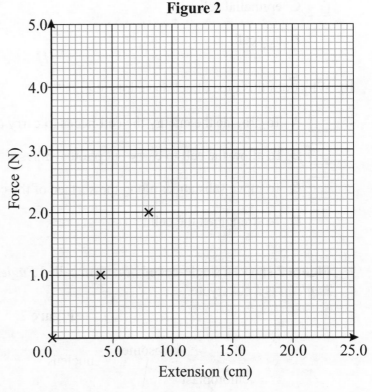

Figure 2

a) Complete the graph in **Figure 2** by plotting the missing data points and drawing a line of best fit.

[3]

b) Using the graph in **Figure 2**, calculate the work done to extend the spring by 10.0 cm.

Work done = ... J

[3]

[Total 6 marks]

2   0.18 J of work is done to stretch a spring.
The spring is stretched elastically by 120 mm.

Calculate the spring constant of the spring. Use an equation from the Equations List.

Spring constant = ... N/m

[Total 3 marks]

Section 23 — Matter

Biology Mixed Questions

1 **Figure 1** shows a type of animal cell. (Grade 1-3)

Figure 1

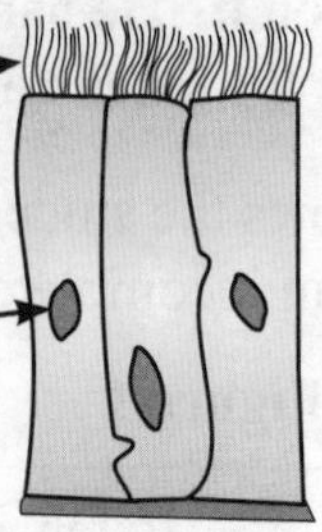

cilia

nucleus

a) What type of cell is the cell in **Figure 1**?

☐ **A** sperm cell

☐ **B** xylem cell

☐ **C** epithelial cell

☐ **D** egg cell

[1]

b) Why does this type of cell have lots of cilia?

☐ **A** To provide the energy the cell needs to carry out its function.

☐ **B** To allow the cell to carry out photosynthesis.

☐ **C** To move substances along the surface of the cell.

☐ **D** To strengthen the cell.

[1]

Figure 2 shows a single-celled organism called *Euglena*, found in pond water. *Euglena* is a eukaryote.

Figure 2

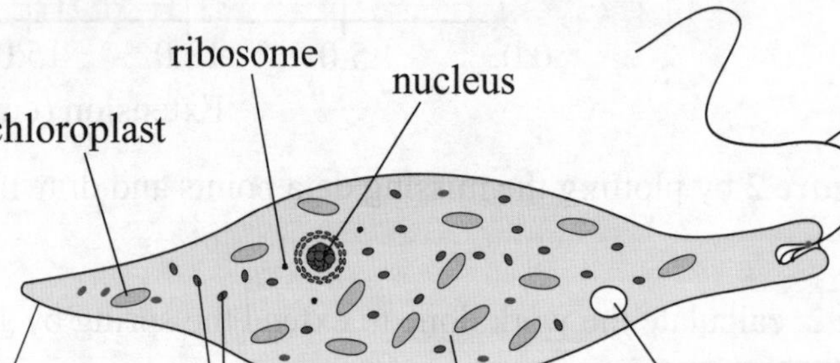

flagellum

ribosome

nucleus

chloroplast

cell membrane

mitochondria

cytoplasm

vacuole

c) Give **one** piece of evidence from **Figure 2** which shows that *Euglena* is a eukaryote and not a prokaryote.

....

[1]

d) Which of the following is an example of a **prokaryote**?

☐ **A** sperm cell   ☐ **B** xylem cell   ☐ **C** fruit fly   ☐ **D** *E. coli* bacterium

[1]

[Total 4 marks]

2   The hormone insulin is made of amino acids.   (Grade 1-3)

a) What type of molecule is made up of amino acids?

☐ **A** a carbohydrate

☐ **B** a protein

☐ **C** a lipid

☐ **D** glycerol

[1]

b) What does insulin control in the human body?

....

[1]

c) What is the name of the condition in which a person's body stops making insulin?

☐ **A** type 1 diabetes

☐ **B** cardiovascular disease

☐ **C** cancer

☐ **D** type 2 diabetes

[1]

[Total 3 marks]

3   Aerobic respiration transfers energy from glucose.   (Grade 3-4)

a) i) Name the sub-cellular structures where aerobic respiration takes place.

....

[1]

ii) Complete the word equation for aerobic respiration.

glucose + ... → .... + water

[2]

Glucose is transported around the body in the blood.

b) Name the liquid component of blood.

....

[1]

c) People with type 2 diabetes have problems with controlling their blood glucose level.
Give **one** factor that increases a person's chance of getting type 2 diabetes.

....

[1]

[Total 5 marks]

4   **Figure 3** shows a plant cell with one of its sub-cellular structures magnified. The overall movement of four molecules into and out of the sub-cellular structure is also shown.

Figure 3

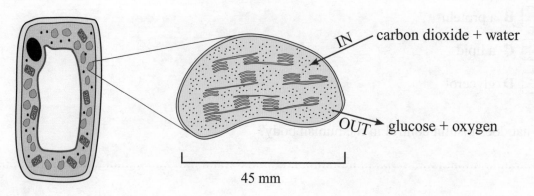

45 mm

a) Look at the movements of carbon dioxide, water, glucose and oxygen in **Figure 3**.
    What reaction do these movements suggest is taking place in the magnified sub-cellular structure?

    ....

    [1]

b) What is the name of the magnified sub-cellular structure in **Figure 3**?

    ....

    [1]

c) The width of the sub-cellular structure when viewed using a microscope is 45 mm.
    What is the width of the magnified image in μm?

    ☐ **A** 45 000 μm   ☐ **B** 0.045 μm   ☐ **C** 4500 μm   ☐ **D** 4.5 μm

    [1]

    The cell in **Figure 3** is from a leaf.

d) Describe how water moves out of a leaf.

    ....

    ....

    [2]

e) What is the name of the process which transports water up a plant and into the leaves?

    ....

    [1]

f) After glucose has been produced by a plant cell, some of it moves out the cell to be
    transported around the plant. What is the name of the transportation process?

    ....

    [1]

    [Total 7 marks]

5   Alcohol dehydrogenase enzymes break down alcohol in the body.

a) Which **one** of the following sentences about enzymes is **true**?

☐ **A** Enzymes speed up chemical reactions in living organisms.

☐ **B** Enzymes are used up in chemical reactions.

☐ **C** Enzymes are products of digestion.

☐ **D** Enzymes are the building blocks of all living organisms.

[1]

A scientist was investigating the effect of pH on the rate of activity of alcohol dehydrogenase. **Figure 4** shows a graph of his results.

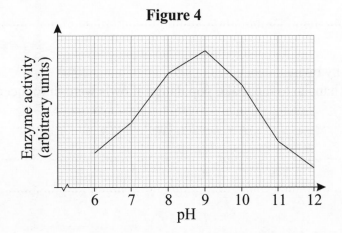

Figure 4

b) What is the optimum pH for the enzyme?

....

[1]

c) Suggest and explain the effect an acid with a pH of 1 would have on the enzyme.

....

....

....

[3]

d) Which of the following statements about alcohol is correct?

☐ **A** Alcohol is a risk factor for several communicable diseases.

☐ **B** Alcohol is a risk factor for lung cancer.

☐ **C** Alcohol is a risk factor for liver disease.

☐ **D** The liver produces alcohol for the rest of the body.

[1]

[Total 6 marks]

6 A scientist is investigating a grassland ecosystem. (Grade 4-5)

a) Give **two** abiotic factors that might affect the amount of grass in this ecosystem.

1. ....

2. ....

[2]

Snakes and mice live in the ecosystem.
The snakes feed on the mice.

b) Explain what might happen to the number of mice in the ecosystem if the number of snakes increased.

....

....

[2]

c) Mice are also eaten by owls.
Explain what might happen to the snake population if owls were introduced to the ecosystem.

....

....

....

[2]

d) Buttercups are a type of plant found in the ecosystem.
Describe a method that the scientist could use to investigate whether the distribution of buttercups changes across the ecosystem.

....

....

....

[3]

e) Some of the mice in the ecosystem are found to have a number of parasites.
What is meant by a parasitic relationship between two organisms?

....

....

[1]

f) The grasses in the ecosystem produce their own biomass using photosynthesis.
What is meant by the term 'biomass'?

....

[1]

[Total 11 marks]

Chemistry Mixed Questions

1   **Figure 1** shows the nuclear symbol of a Group 1 element.

Figure 1

a) Write the name of the element that the symbol in **Figure 1** represents.

....
                                                                                                    [1]

b) Name another element in the same group as the element shown in **Figure 1**.

....
                                                                                                    [1]

c) The nucleus of an atom contains protons and neutrons. Draw **one** line from each of these
    particles to show how many there are in an atom of the element shown in **Figure 1**.

    Particle   **Number in one atom of Li**

                                          3

         proton   7

                                          4

         neutron   1

                                                                                                    [2]

d) The element in **Figure 1** is a metal. Which of the following
    diagrams shows the structure of a metal? Tick **one** box.

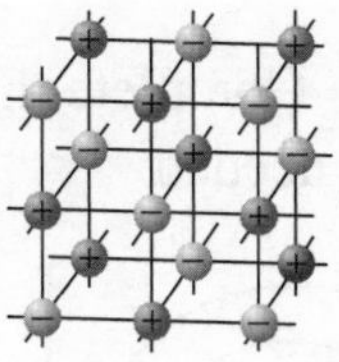

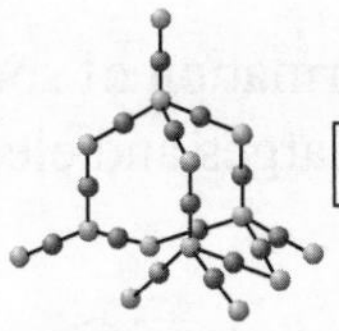

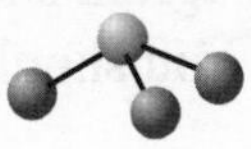

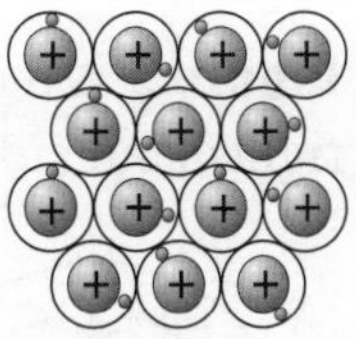

                                                                                                    [1]

e) LiOH is produced when the element in **Figure 1** reacts with water.
    Complete the sentence below. Use a word from the box.

    | oxide | hydroxide | carbonate |

    When a Group 1 element reacts with water a metal .... is formed.
                                                                                                    [1]

                                                                                      [Total 6 marks]

2   Hydrochloric acid and sodium hydroxide react in a neutralisation reaction.

a) A student carries out an experiment to find the volume of hydrochloric acid needed to neutralise 25 cm³ of sodium hydroxide. She does the experiment three times. Her results are in **Figure 2**.

Complete **Figure 2** to show the mean volume of hydrochloric acid needed.

Repeat	1	2	3	mean
Volume (cm³)	35.60	35.90	35.75	....

Figure 2

[2]

b) Calculate the uncertainty of the mean.
   Use the equation: uncertainty = range ÷ 2

Uncertainty = ... cm³

[2]

c) The products of the reaction between hydrochloric acid and sodium hydroxide are sodium chloride and water. Complete the equation below to show this reaction.

.... + NaOH → .... + H₂O

[2]

d) The student measures the pH of the sodium hydroxide at the start of the experiment. She then measures the pH as the hydrochloric acid is added and the pH at the end of the reaction.

Describe how the pH of the reaction mixture would change during the experiment.

....

....

....

[3]

e) **Figure 3** is a dot and cross diagram showing the formation of sodium chloride. Complete the right-hand side of **Figure 3**. You should add any charges and electrons that are needed.

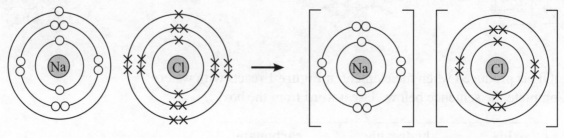

Figure 3

[2]

f) State the type of bonding in sodium chloride.

....

[1]

[Total 12 marks]

3   Crude oil contains hydrocarbons of different sizes.

a) **Figure 4** shows some physical properties of hydrocarbons.
Tick **one** box in each column to show whether each is a property
of short or long hydrocarbons.

	Higher boiling points	**Easier to ignite**	**More viscous**
Short hydrocarbons			
Long hydrocarbons			

Figure 4

[3]

b) Hydrocarbons are used as fuels. What gas is released if they burn completely in air?

....

[1]

c) Burning hydrocarbons often produces pollutants.
Give **one** example of an alternative, cleaner fuel that could be used to power vehicles.

....

[1]

[Total 5 marks]

4   Chlorine is a Group 7 element with seven electrons in its outer shell.
Chlorine exists as molecules of Cl_2.

a) Complete the dot-and-cross diagram below to show the bonding in Cl_2.
You only need to show the outer electron shells.

Cl   Cl

[2]

b) Which of the following **best** describes the structure of chlorine?
Tick **one** box.

▢ **A** Giant ionic lattice   ▢ **C** Simple molecular substance

▢ **B** Giant covalent structure   ▢ **D** Fullerene

[1]

c) Describe a test you could carry out to identify chlorine.
Include any observations you would expect to make.

....

....

[2]

[Total 5 marks]

194

5   Oxygen atoms have the electronic structure 2.6. (Grade 4-5)

a) State which group of the periodic table oxygen is in.
Explain your answer with reference to the electronic structure of oxygen.

Group: ....

Explanation: ....
....
[2]

b) Oxygen can react to form oxide ions. Predict the charge on an oxide ion.
Give a reason for your answer.

Charge: ....

Reason: ....
[2]

[Total 4 marks]

6   A student reacts four different metals with dilute sulfuric acid. He controls all
other variables to make sure that the test is fair. He collects the gas given off by
each reaction in a gas syringe. **Figure 5** shows all four reactions after 30 seconds. (Grade 4-5)

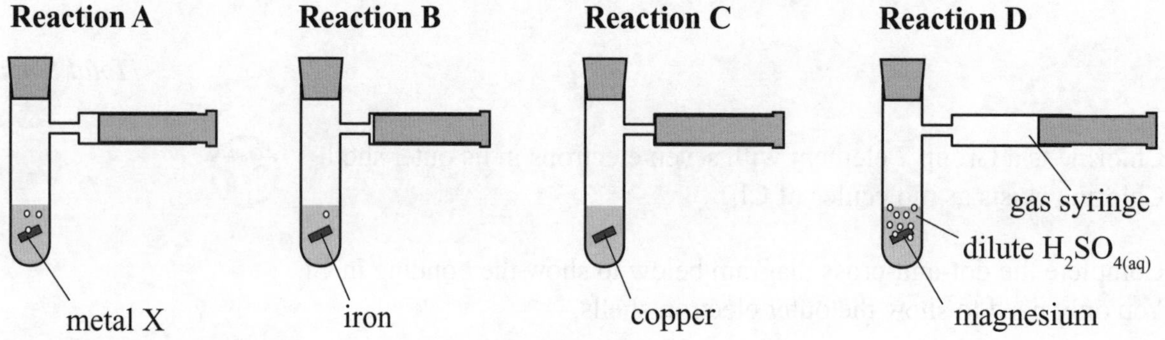

Reaction A   **Reaction B**   **Reaction C**   **Reaction D**

gas syringe

dilute $H_2SO_{4(aq)}$

metal X   iron   copper   magnesium

Figure 5

a) Name the gas that is being collected in the gas syringes.

....
[1]

b) Which reaction, **A**, **B**, **C** or **D**, contains the **most reactive** metal?
Explain how you can tell.

....
....
....
[3]

c) Use your knowledge of the reactivity series to suggest
a possible identity for metal X. Tick **one** box.

☐ **A** Zinc   ☐ **B** Gold   ☐ **C** Potassium   ☐ **D** Sodium
[1]

[Total 5 marks]

Chemistry Mixed Questions

7 When sodium hydrogen carbonate reacts with ethanoic acid, the temperature of the surroundings decreases.

(Grade 4-5)

a) Is this reaction endothermic or exothermic?

....

[1]

b) Will the energy of the products be higher or lower than the energy of the reactants?

....

[1]

c) What effect will increasing the concentration of ethanoic acid have on the rate of the reaction? Give a reason for your answer.

Effect: ....

Reason: ....

....

[3]

[Total 5 marks]

8 Aluminium and iron can be obtained by extracting them from their ores. Both metals can also be obtained from recycling aluminium and iron items.

(Grade 4-5)

Material	Extraction process	Energy saved by recycling
Aluminium	Electrolysis	Around 95%
Iron	Reduction with carbon	Around 60%

Figure 6

a) Look at **Figure 6**. Suggest whether the extraction of aluminium or iron will be more expensive. Give a reason for your answer.

Extraction process: ....

Reason: ....

....

....

....

[4]

b) **Figure 6** shows that energy is saved when aluminium and iron are obtained by recycling rather than extracting them from their ores. Give **two** other advantages of recycling metals.

1 ....

2 ....

[2]

[Total 6 marks]

9 A student is using paper chromatography to analyse a substance.
Figure 7 shows the chromatogram produced by the experiment.

PRACTICAL

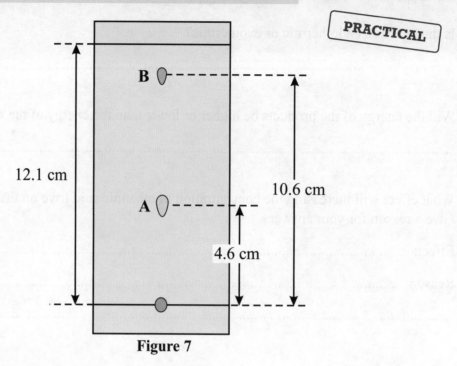

Figure 7

a) Identify the **stationary phase** in this experiment.

....

[1]

b) Use **Figure 7** to calculate the R_f values for spots **A** and **B**.
Give your answers to 2 significant figures.

Use the equation: $R_f = \dfrac{\text{distance travelled by solute}}{\text{distance travelled by solvent}}$

R_f of **A** = ...

R_f of **B** = ...

[2]

c) From **Figure 7**, how can you tell that the student's sample contains
a substance that doesn't dissolve in the mobile phase?

....

[1]

d) The student concludes that her sample is a mixture. Explain what is meant by the term 'mixture'.

....

....

[1]

e) The mixture contains a number of liquids with similar boiling points.
Name a technique that the student could use to separate the different components in the mixture.

....

[1]

[Total 6 marks]

10 A student added an excess of zinc oxide (ZnO) to dilute hydrochloric acid (HCl). They reacted to produced zinc chloride, a soluble salt.

   a) In addition to the zinc chloride, one other product is formed by this reaction. Name the other product of the reaction.

   ....

   [1]

   b) Give the chemical formula of zinc chloride.

   ....

   [1]

   c) Describe how you could produce pure, dry crystals of zinc chloride from the reaction mixture after the reaction had finished.

   ....

   ....

   ....

   ....

   ....

   [4]

   [Total 6 marks]

11* The structure and bonding of substances affects their properties.

	Hardness	Melting point	Conducts electricity?
Diamond	Hard	High	No
Graphite	Soft	High	Yes

Figure 8

Explain how the structure and bonding of diamond and graphite give them the properties listed in **Figure 8**.
Your answer should include details of how the atoms are arranged and how they're held together.

....

....

....

....

....

....

....

[Total 6 marks]

Physics Mixed Questions

1 Infrared radiation is a type of electromagnetic wave. (Grade 1-3)

a) Which of the following statements about infrared radiation is **true**? Tick **one** box.

☐ **A** Infrared radiation is a transverse wave.

☐ **B** Infrared radiation is a longitudinal wave.

☐ **C** Infrared radiation travels slower in a vacuum than gamma radiation.

☐ **D** Infrared radiation transfers matter, not energy.

[1]

b) Name **one** type of electromagnetic wave that has a lower frequency than infrared radiation.

....
[1]

c) Give **one** use of infrared radiation.

....
[1]

[Total 3 marks]

2 A kettle is used to heat some water until it starts to boil. (Grade 1-3)

a) Use phrases from the box below to complete the passage about water.

as dense as	closer together	denser than	less dense than	further apart

Water vapour is a gas. Water vapour is .... liquid water.

The particles in water vapour are .... than in liquid water.
[2]

b) How does the energy stored in the water particles' energy stores and the water's temperature change when the water is **boiling**? Tick **one** box for the correct row of the table.

		Energy	Temperature
☐	**A**	No change	Increases
☐	**B**	Increases	No change
☐	**C**	No change	No change
☐	**D**	Increases	Increases

[1]

[Total 3 marks]

3 A cyclist is riding their bike. (Grade 3-4)

a) What is the typical speed of a cyclist? Tick **one** box.

☐ **A** 0.25 m/s

☐ **B** 5.5 m/s

☐ **C** 14 m/s

☐ **D** 20 m/s

[1]

b) The cyclist accelerates to this typical speed from rest.
The cyclist has an average acceleration of 0.55 m/s^2.
Calculate the time it takes the cyclist to reach this typical speed.
Use the equation:

time taken = change in velocity ÷ acceleration

Time taken = ... s

[2]

c) A friend of the cyclist has a trundle wheel and a stopwatch.
A trundle wheel is used for measuring large distances.
Describe how they could use this equipment to find the average speed of the cyclist.

....

....

....

....

[3]

[Total 6 marks]

4 A scientist is working with a radioactive source. For safety reasons, the source is kept in a box with a thick lead lining when it is not being used. (Grade 3-4)

a) It would be dangerous to keep the source in a similar box made of wood.
Suggest what type of radiation the source emits.

....

[1]

b) Explain how storing the source in a box with a thick lead lining keeps the scientist safe.
You should refer to the negative effects the radiation could have on the health of the scientist.

....

....

....

[2]

[Total 3 marks]

Physics Mixed Questions

5 A driver is travelling along a motorway. She records the total distance she has travelled every 5 minutes. She uses the information she collects to draw a distance/time graph for her journey.

Grade 3-4

a) State what quantity the gradient of a distance/time graph shows.

....

[1]

b) She drives for a total of 25.0 minutes.
   Her average speed is 25.0 m/s.
   Calculate the total distance travelled during this time.
   Use the equation:

$$\text{distance travelled} = \text{average speed} \times \text{time}$$

Distance travelled = ... m

[3]

c) The driver pulls off the motorway and drives at a lower speed.
   State what effect this will have on the driver's thinking distance and braking distance.

....

....

[2]

[Total 6 marks]

6 The equation below shows a technetium (Tc) nucleus emitting a gamma ray.

Grade 3-4

$$^{99}_{43}\text{Tc} \rightarrow {}^{A}_{43}\text{Tc} + {}^{B}_{0}\gamma$$

a) Determine the values of A and B.

A = ...

B = ...

[2]

b) Suggest why gamma radiation is emitted from the technetium nucleus following radioactive decay.

....

[1]

c) Suggest **one** other way that electromagnetic radiation could be emitted from an atom.

....

....

[1]

[Total 4 marks]

Physics Mixed Questions

7   A student varies the current through a fixed resistor. He measures the potential difference across the fixed resistor for different values of current. Using his results, he plots an *I-V* graph for the fixed resistor.

a) Sketch the *I-V* graph the student would expect to get on the axes in **Figure 1**.

Figure 1

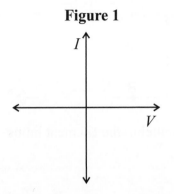

[2]

b) The student finds the resistance of the fixed resistor to be 6 Ω.

  i) Give the equation that links potential difference, current and resistance.

  ....
  [1]

  ii) Calculate the current through the fixed resistor when the potential difference across it is 18 V.

  Current = ... A
  [3]
  [Total 6 marks]

8   **Figure 2** contains information about three atoms.

Figure 2

	Mass number	Atomic number
Atom A	32	17
Atom B	33	17
Atom C	32	16

a) State which of the two atoms in **Figure 2** are isotopes of the same element. Explain your answer.

....

....

....
[2]

b) Atom B emits a beta particle. Atom B then emits a gamma ray.
The gamma ray travels at a speed of 3×10^8 m/s and has a frequency of 1.5×10^{19} Hz.

  i) Give the equation that links wave speed, wavelength and frequency.

  ....
  [1]

  ii) Calculate the wavelength of the gamma ray.

  Wavelength = ... m
  [3]
  [Total 6 marks]

9   A student creates the circuit shown in **Figure 3**.
    Three points are labelled on the circuit as A, B and C.

Figure 3

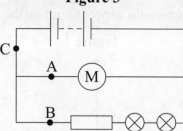

a) Name **one** component that is in parallel to the filament bulbs.

....

[1]

b) The current at Point A is 5 A. The current at Point B is 2 A. Calculate the current at Point C.

Current at Point C = ... A

[1]

c) The student notices that if the circuit is left on for a long period of time, the resistor gets hot.
Explain what causes this in terms of energy transfers.

....

....

....

[2]

[Total 4 marks]

10   Heater A and Heater B are two electric heaters. It takes 340 s
    for Heater A to heat 0.50 kg of water from 25 °C to 45 °C.

a) Calculate the energy transferred to the thermal energy store of the water.
The specific heat capacity of water is 4200 J/kg °C. Use an equation from the Equations List.

Change in thermal energy = ... J

[3]

b) It takes Heater B 170 s to heat 0.50 kg of water from 25 °C to 45 °C. You can assume both
heaters are 100 % efficient. You can also assume all the energy is transferred to the water.

State which of the two heaters has the higher power rating. Explain your answer.

....

....

....

[3]

[Total 6 marks]

11 A child is playing with a remote-controlled toy car.

a) The car has a mass of 1.0 kg. The car is travelling at 6.0 m/s.

i) Give the equation that links kinetic energy, mass and speed.

....

[1]

ii) Calculate the amount of energy in the car's kinetic energy store.

Energy = ... J

[2]

b) The car is powered by an electric motor.
The total energy transferred to the motor in 2 minutes is 0.75 kJ.

i) Give the equation that links energy transferred, charge moved and potential difference.

....

[1]

ii) The potential difference across the electric motor is 2.5 V.
Calculate the total charge that passes through the motor during these 2 minutes.

Charge = ... C

[3]

c) The car has a bar magnet attached to the back of it. The child places a toy trailer next to the magnet. This is shown in **Figure 4**. The trailer is made from a material that contains iron.

When the car moves, the trailer moves with the car. Explain why.

Figure 4

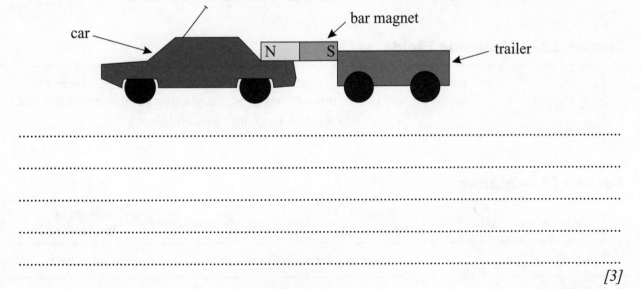

....

....

....

....

....

[3]

[Total 10 marks]

Physics Mixed Questions

The Periodic Table

Periods

	Group 1	Group 2													Group 3	Group 4	Group 5	Group 6	Group 7	Group 0
1								1 H Hydrogen 1													4 He Helium 2
2	7 Li Lithium 3	9 Be Beryllium 4														11 B Boron 5	12 C Carbon 6	14 N Nitrogen 7	16 O Oxygen 8	19 F Fluorine 9	20 Ne Neon 10
3	23 Na Sodium 11	24 Mg Magnesium 12														27 Al Aluminium 13	28 Si Silicon 14	31 P Phosphorus 15	32 S Sulfur 16	35.5 Cl Chlorine 17	40 Ar Argon 18
4	39 K Potassium 19	40 Ca Calcium 20	45 Sc Scandium 21	48 Ti Titanium 22	51 V Vanadium 23	52 Cr Chromium 24	55 Mn Manganese 25	56 Fe Iron 26	59 Co Cobalt 27	59 Ni Nickel 28	63.5 Cu Copper 29	65 Zn Zinc 30	70 Ga Gallium 31	73 Ge Germanium 32	75 As Arsenic 33	79 Se Selenium 34	80 Br Bromine 35	84 Kr Krypton 36
5	85 Rb Rubidium 37	88 Sr Strontium 38	89 Y Yttrium 39	91 Zr Zirconium 40	93 Nb Niobium 41	96 Mo Molybdenum 42	98 Tc Technetium 43	101 Ru Ruthenium 44	103 Rh Rhodium 45	106 Pd Palladium 46	108 Ag Silver 47	112 Cd Cadmium 48	115 In Indium 49	119 Sn Tin 50	122 Sb Antimony 51	128 Te Tellurium 52	127 I Iodine 53	131 Xe Xenon 54
6	133 Cs Caesium 55	137 Ba Barium 56	139 La Lanthanum 57	178 Hf Hafnium 72	181 Ta Tantalum 73	184 W Tungsten 74	186 Re Rhenium 75	190 Os Osmium 76	192 Ir Iridium 77	195 Pt Platinum 78	197 Au Gold 79	201 Hg Mercury 80	204 Tl Thallium 81	207 Pb Lead 82	209 Bi Bismuth 83	209 Po Polonium 84	210 At Astatine 85	222 Rn Radon 86
7	223 Fr Francium 87	226 Ra Radium 88	227 Ac Actinium 89	261 Rf Rutherfordium 104	262 Db Dubnium 105	266 Sg Seaborgium 106	264 Bh Bohrium 107	277 Hs Hassium 108	268 Mt Meitnerium 109	271 Ds Darmstadtium 110	272 Rg Roentgenium 111							

Relative atomic mass →

Atomic number →

Equations

Here are some equations you might find useful for the Physics sections — you'll be given these in the exams.

Section 17 — Motion, Forces and Conservation of Energy

$v^2 - u^2 = 2 \times a \times x$	(final velocity)^2 − (initial velocity)^2 = 2 × acceleration × distance

Section 21 — Electricity and Circuits

$E = I \times V \times t$	energy transferred = current × potential difference × time

Make sure you understand all the equations on this page, and you're happy using and rearranging them.

Section 22 — Magnetic Fields

$V_p \times I_p = V_s \times I_s$	potential difference across primary coil × current in primary coil = potential difference across secondary coil × current in secondary coil (for transformers with 100% efficiency)

Section 23 — Matter

$\Delta Q = m \times c \times \Delta\theta$	change in thermal energy = mass × specific heat capacity × change in temperature
$Q = m \times L$	thermal energy for a change of state = mass × specific latent heat
$E = \frac{1}{2} \times k \times x^2$	energy transferred in stretching = 0.5 × spring constant × (extension)^2